Shirley,

Wonders never cease —
I have become an arthor!

Fred Bedelle Jr

★ WITH ALL ★
DELIBERATE SPEED

★ WITH ALL ★

DELIBERATE SPEED

THE STORY OF SCHOOL DESEGREGATION IN KNOXVILLE, TENNESSEE

FRED BEDELLE JR.

PLUMBLINE
MEDIA

Printed in the United States of America

16   15   14   13   12   1   2   3   4   5

Library of Congress Control Number: 2012947152

ISBN: 978-1-937824-07-5

Cover painting courtesy of Tom Underwood and artist Ron Williams
Cover design by Joey McNair
Page design by Holly Jones

PLUMBLINE MEDIA, LLC
415 BRIDGE STREET
FRANKLIN, TENNESSEE 37064
615-442-8582
WWW.PLUMBLINEMEDIA.NET

To
My wife, Norma
Daughters, Donna and Frieda
and
In memory of Sam F. Fowler Jr.

CONTENTS

FOREWORD

D R. FRED BEDELLE JR. HAS WRITTEN a very interesting and informative book about the history of the desegregation of the city schools of Knoxville. I am honored that he has asked me to write a foreword to this fascinating book.

Dr. Bedelle has spent his career in education and has always been one of the most highly respected educators in the state of Tennessee. He has firsthand knowledge of the events about which he has written.

I, too, remember this period well. My late father, John J. Duncan Sr., was city law director for a little over three years and mayor of Knoxville for almost six years. His time at these two posts covered the nine full years from January 1956 through December 1964.

Those same years represented my life from age eight to age seventeen. I was a student at Chilhowee Elementary School and Holston, which was then both a junior and senior high school. They were city public schools and, in my opinion, were great schools with outstanding, dedicated teachers.

In some ways, I grew up at city hall. Even after my father went to Congress in January 1965, I stayed in Knoxville to graduate from Holston. Then I attended the University of Tennessee for the next four years, graduating in 1969. So I remember well all of the years about which Dr. Bedelle has written, and I remember all the people.

Congressmen John J. Duncan Sr. and John J. Duncan Jr. on the campaign circuit. Photo courtesy of John J. Duncan Jr.

My father was a part-time assistant attorney general for Kno County from 1947 to 1956. In that position, he worked and becam friends with Carl Cowan. Judge Robert Taylor was the lone feder: judge in Knoxville from 1949 until 1985. I appeared in his court man times after I started practicing law in 1973.

I was very proud of my father's record on civil rights. I ca remember him taking me as a small boy in the mid 1950s into blac churches where he spoke. This was unusual for a white politician in th South in those years.

Being Presbyterian, my brother and sisters and I, when we wer young, were supposed to be very quiet in church. I remember my shoc when I first saw grown men shouting out "Amen!" and other encour aging words in an African-American church.

My father was a hero to many in the black community i Knoxville. As mayor, he traveled to New York City, Cleveland, an possibly other places to ask national chains to allow the integration o their stores in Knoxville. While there were problems here, and reall in every section of the country, Knoxville received an All-America

City Award from *Look* magazine in 1962 in large part for the peaceful way integration was handled here. *Look* magazine at that time had a circulation in the millions.

I remember meetings in our home in the Holston Hills section of East Knoxville with black leaders such as Sarah Moore Greene, Rev. W. T. Crutcher, Rev. Robert James, Tommy Moore, Clarence Hardin, and Willie Whitelow, who was called the "Mayor of Mechanicsville."

In those years, Raymond Smith, the black maitre d' at the Andrew Johnson Hotel, was like a member of

Congressman John J. Duncan Jr.
Photo courtesy of John J. Duncan Jr.

our family. In fact, many years later, we made him an "honorary Duncan" at one of our family reunions. Raymond was a real leader among many of the lower-income blacks in Knoxville.

My father was a conservative Republican who received about 95 percent of the vote in the black precincts of Knoxville in three races for mayor. As a conservative, he believed in the inherent worth of every individual and believed in freedom.

My father could not have helped lead the peaceful integration of the city schools, however, without support from many white citizens. I remember most of those who are mentioned in this book, but especially T. Mack Blackburn, C. R. "Doc" McClain, Dr. John Burkhart, and most of the other school board and school officials named.

Dr. Bedelle has performed a great public service in writing this thoroughly researched book. I hope many people will read it, learn from it, and realize that no matter how big or how bad problems may seem, there are always people of goodwill trying to do what is right.

John J. Duncan Jr.
Congressman
Second Congressional District of Tennessee

PREFACE
AND
ACKNOWLEDGMENTS

IN EARLY MARCH 2010 I RECEIVED a phone call from Don Ferguson, executive director, US District Court Historical Society. He was interested in organizing an audiotaping with Sam F. Fowler Jr. and me to discuss the *Josephine Goss v. Knoxville Board of Education* school desegregation case. The taping was to recount what Sam and I could remember about the case. We were the only two individuals still living that had major roles in the hearings. Sam's father, Frank Fowler, was the board of education's attorney from the beginning of the case. Sam had been associated with the case, and later took on a major role as his father entered semiretirement in 1967.

I was employed by the Knoxville Board of Education in 1963 and was assigned the role of representing the board in the hearings and the desegregation action of the system in 1965. Sam and I worked very closely for the remainder of the litigation. When Sam Fowler retired, he gave me his father's desegregation files. All of these events and the discussion following the taping are the genesis of this book.

The assistance, advice, and support given by Sam Fowler and Don Ferguson were invaluable. When Sam died before the book was finished, I not only lost a good friend, but a major contributor. The loss of my "in house" translator of the legal language was a major bump in completing the book.

Dr. Fred Bedelle Jr. and Sam F. Fowler Jr. at the audiotaping session of their memories of the Goss *case. This taping is preserved in the archives of the Federal Court of the Eastern District of Tennessee.* Photo courtesy of Don Ferguson.

Don Ferguson knows the federal court system, especially the Eastern District of Tennessee, better than anyone I have ever met. This knowledge and understanding of the system and the individuals, judges, and lawyers comes from his experiences as chief deputy clerk of court, as a reporter (covering many of the court proceedings), and as city editor for the *Knoxville News-Sentinel*. He has given guidance about writing a book, made available the docket sheet of the *Goss* case, and throughout the research phase answered many, many questions. His encouragement kept me from quitting on several occasions. I am deeply indebted.

After committing to write the book, I went to the one individual that has written more about the black history of Knoxville than anyone I know, Robert "Bob" Booker. He treated me as if we were very close friends, listened to what I had to say about my proposed book, and responded with, "Wait a minute, I have something you might be interested in." A few minutes later, he returned with seventy-four pages of newspaper clippings on the subject of "school desegregation in Knoxville." That bundle of clippings has saved me hours and hours of staring with weak eyes into a microfilm reader for newspaper articles.

That was just the beginning of Bob's assistance with this book. His time and help with a myriad of questions and the reading of an embarrassing draft copy makes him my friend for life. He could easily qualify for co-author of this account.

Being married to a retired English teacher/librarian can't hurt, if you don't know anything about writing a book. Norma's patience, expertise, and persistent "Can I do anything to help?" really made her the driving force to finish. Our daughters, Donna Folkner and Frieda Brown, provided support by being my proofreaders and computer experts. On occasion they assisted by doing research in the National Archives in Morrow, Georgia.

Both of our daughters lived through the desegregation years as teenagers and have less than pleasant memories of phone calls and disparaging remarks about their father that are not included in this account.

This period of time in my professional life was exciting, and I needed all the help I could get to do the job that I had been assigned. Colleagues too numerous to mention helped. I received both the blame and credit for *our* efforts. I am indebted.

Interviews with Avon W. Rollins, Sarah Moore Greene, State Representative Joe Armstrong, Dr. Paul Kelley, Ruth Benn, Dr. Robert Harvey, Carroll Grubbs, Tom Underwood, Wanda Moody, Dessa Blair, Connie Mills, Frank Bowden, Raleigh Wynn, A. B. Coleman, Margaret Gaither, Josephine Goss Sims, Thomas Goss, and a host of others are

Robert "Bob" Booker, civil rights activist, historian, writer, and a major contributor to this book.
Photo courtesy of Robert Booker.

all a part of this story and the process of school desegregation i Knoxville. Some of these individuals will be mentioned in the book However, many individuals interviewed who contributed informatio that made the account a much more meaningful story will not b mentioned. This story would not have been possible without this infor mation. I am most grateful.

This is the story of years of desegregation activities and a tribute t those dedicated and committed individuals—including plaintiff community members, lawyers, board members, and school personnel– who gave of themselves and stayed the course.

I think of the two years of writing this story as "grabbing a tiger b the tail." I had to hold on or the other end of the tiger would have bee more difficult to deal with.

Because of the help and encouragement of a myriad of friends, I ar better for the experience. Now I have a family larger than any I ever ha growing up and friends that came out of nowhere.

In all this murky atmosphere of pessimism and doubt there is but one faint beacon light of hope—the school. Civilization is indissolubly bound up in the ever lengthening period of immaturity. Education, which is the guardian of civilization, owes its efficiency to the same factor. In return for this priceless advantage, education must in some way make up for nature's lack of foresight. It can do this in part by replacing ignorance and mystery with knowledge, in part by insuring an environment that is free from suggestions of evil, and in part by developing the highest ideals of purity and honor. At best the task is Herculean; but if education fails in this one supreme test, it needs no prophet's vision to perceive that human progress, for which education stands sponsor, will sooner or later end in a cul-de-sac.

—William Chandler Bagley
The Educative Process, 1922

★ WITH ALL ★
DELIBERATE SPEED

INTRODUCTION

DESEGREGATION OF SCHOOL SYSTEMS in the South, after the 1954 *Brown v. Topeka Board of Education* decision and the subsequent decision in 1955, took many forms; caused varying degrees of interruptions; and involved all schools, teachers, and parents, as well as governmental officials and politicians. The *Brown I* (1954) and the *Brown II* (1955) decisions produced more significant changes in schooling in the South than any event in the history of public education with the possible exceptions of the two world wars. How the actual desegregation of schools happened and with what speed depended on racial conditions in each state, school system, and community involved.

Knoxville, Tennessee, is a city located in the center of what has become known as Appalachia. Historically, Appalachia was known by coal mines, hill farming, poverty, "hillbillies," and moonshine. In his 1947 book, *Inside USA*, John Gunther referred to Knoxville as "the ugliest city in America." Several years later, as the city was preparing for the challenge of hosting the World's Fair in 1980, the *Wall Street Journal* labeled it a "scruffy little city . . . on the Tennessee River." It obviously improved its image beyond ugly and scruffy because the World's Fair became a reality and a success.

Knoxville had its share of the stress, prejudice, concerns, problems, and discomfort with the desegregation process. In addition to improving its reputation as an ugly city, Knoxville managed to avoid the turmoil with the school desegregation process that engulfed some communities in the South.

This is not to say that Knoxville welcomed school desegregation with open arms. It did not! Knoxville reacted much like other communities, North and South, faced with effects of the *Brown* decisions; but for reasons particular to this community, school desegregation was different. This difference probably can be attributed to the time when the case was filed, the approach taken by the board's attorney, the attitude of the board as it related to their constitutional duties, and the leadership of community leaders and school personnel.

Much has been written about desegregation of schools in the South as well as the court cases *(Brown I* and *Brown II)* that ended the legal practice of "separate but equal" in education. The court case that accelerated the desegregation of the Knoxville city schools has had little exposure. *Josephine Goss et al. v. The Board of Education of the City of Knoxville, Tennessee, et al.* has received documentation by authors such as Dr. Patricia E. Brake, Merrill Proudfoot, Robert Booker, Dr. Paul Kelley, and others who have commented on the desegregation efforts of this area and the South. However, the story of school desegregation in Knoxville from the filing of the complaint to the Supreme Court's final ruling, has not been documented.

Robert "Bob" Booker has written extensively regarding individuals involved in the various desegregation and civil rights efforts in Knoxville. He has also related other events and actions of personalities in the black community that have made a difference in the social order of Knoxville. His writings serve to embellish this account on a personal basis.

Many individuals in Knoxville, black and white, were involved in the desegregation of the Knoxville school system. Like all other members of the community, they experienced the reluctance of the white community to desegregate, and the urgency of the black community to "get on with it," but wanted no part of the disruptive events that many communities were experiencing. These individuals have not had their "day in the sun." The account of this court case, if I did my job, should serve to highlight their contributions to the school system and to the community.

This documentation of the *Goss* case is based on court records and official Knoxville Board of Education minutes that reflect the reaction of board members to the court's orders. Newspaper accounts and interviews with individuals involved in the process were used to give personal and community reactions.

My goals have been to develop the context of the events and the time period in which they occurred; identify some of the individuals and groups that were actively participating in the process; and relate how the media, the Knoxville Board of Education's actions, and the rulings of the court were the forces that successfully desegregated a segregated school system in a very orderly manner. The court case and the subsequent board actions should be of special interest to those individuals wanting to delve into the history of desegregation in this southern region and perhaps students who want to understand a little of the history of desegregation.

Without the persistent, scared, sometimes angry, but level-headed actions of individuals on both sides of the issue, the ending would have been the same, but the process would have been much more disruptive and probably not as successful. Knoxville owes a deep sense of appreciation and gratitude to these individuals, even though most of the people living in Knoxville now have never heard their names.

With the effects of time and events that have passed since the case ended, I must acknowledge that success is in the eye of the beholder. Depending on the definition of "success," this account leaves room for justified criticism on all sides of the issue.

I was deeply involved during the last years of the case as an employee of the Knoxville Board of Education, but mention of my role will be recounted only by job title (director of research, assistant superintendent, etc.) or simply staff member. Every member of the central office staff contributed to the process over the years of litigation and should be appreciated for their efforts.

The Board of Education of the City of Knoxville, Tennessee, will be "the board" in this story. "Desegregation" was the word used to describe the process of mixing the races at the time of the *Brown* decision, but later in the process it was referred to as "integration," and at the end of this account it had become "unitary." These terms will be used as they appear in the media and court documents. References to African American individuals or groups will be the words "black," "negro," "colored," or "Negro," as they appear in media and court documents at the time of reference.

I interviewed dozens of individuals to establish context and to get reactions to specific events. Some of these individuals are named, but many teachers, principals, former students, public officials, and others who contributed information that made the account a much more meaningful story are not mentioned by name.

The core of this account is the docket sheet of the *Goss* case. Briefs and correspondence between attorneys from the files of Carl Cowan, Frank Fowler, and Sam Fowler provided insight into the roles the attorneys played outside the courtroom. Board minutes provided the official record of board action taken to comply with the mandates of *Brown*. Interviews with individuals involved in the process, by employment or community interest, gave the human side of the efforts. Newspaper articles related most of the information to which the community had access.

Information from the Calvin M. McClung Historical Collection; Knox County Archives; National Archives, Southeast Region, in Morrow, Georgia; the Knox County Museum of Education; and the Beck Cultural Exchange Center was invaluable. The staffs of all these organizations were courteous and professional. Their assistance was essential to the completion of this account.

CHAPTER 1

BEFORE 1959

T HE MAJOR DESEGREGATION CASE in Knoxville, *Josephine Goss et al. v. The Board of Education of the City of Knoxville, Tennessee, et al.*, was filed on December 11, 1959. Two years earlier *Dianne Ward et al. v. The Board of Education of the City of Knoxville, Tennessee, et al.* had been filed. The reasons supporting these complaints existed long before that date. A short history of the events relating to school desegregation leading up to the filing of the *Ward* and *Goss* cases is necessary in order to establish context for this account and the appropriate setting for the story.

Tennessee has had a long history of racial segregation. It was a slave state. After the end of the Civil War and continuing into the 1950s, Tennessee legislatures enacted a series of statutes that legalized racial segregation. These "Jim Crow" laws required segregation in the social and community life of all citizens of the state.

As early as 1870, the Tennessee Constitution was amended to prohibit interracial marriage. In 1875 a state statute gave specific rights to hotel keepers, carriers of passengers, and keepers of places of amusement to exclude *any person the proprietor desired*. Railroad companies were required in a statute passed in 1881 to furnish separate cars for "colored" passengers. In 1885 proprietors of theaters, parks, shows, and other places of public amusements were given the right to develop separate accommodations for whites and blacks. In 1905 a law was passed requiring all streetcars to designate a portion of each car for white and "colored."

In 1932 the state code was amended to define as "negro" any person with any "negro" blood. The statute did not mention Native American blood or any of the other mixtures that could have been found in the state at this time. The state code was changed four times in 1932 in order to enforce segregation. This new code prohibited racially mixed couples (of all ethnic blood) from living together as man and wife; required separate facilities for blacks and whites in mental institutions; required all public transportation to be segregated; and required separate washrooms for blacks and whites in the mines.[1] These restrictions were aimed at controlling social and community life, mainly of the adult population.

There was another set of laws aimed at the young folks of the state. These laws required segregation for the education programs. In 1866, one year after the end of the Civil War, the Tennessee Legislature passed an act requiring separate school systems for white and black children. In 1869 the Tennessee Constitution was amended, barring racial integration in all public schools. However, the article did grant all citizens of the state, regardless of color, the right to attend the University of Tennessee, but only in separate facilities from those used by white students.[2] In 1901 the legislature passed a law prohibiting integration of private colleges.

In the 1870s several acts were passed to enforce the dual system. One of the early acts required schools for white and "colored" students to be separate. Later legislation mandated the management standards for both races to be similar, but in separate facilities, and "white and colored persons shall not be taught in the same school . . ." It became an offense punishable by a fine of fifty dollars or imprisonment from thirty to sixty days for any teacher to teach an integrated class. In 1925 a statute was passed that required separate elementary and high schools be maintained for Negro and white children. In 1932 an act was passed to require segregated high schools.[3]

Knoxville established a public school system in 1870. The system was segregated as required by Tennessee state law. All schools in the Knoxville school system were designed as neighborhood schools. This meant that students either walked to school or provided their own transportation.

Since residential communities were predominately either white or black, students in some areas found themselves walking by a school of the other race to get to the school of their race. This was especially true with the upper grades. Junior and senior high schools were centrally located and served the entire city or, as the population grew, large segments of the city.

As vocational programs were introduced into the curriculum they were developed for traditional black occupations and/or white occupations. For example, Fulton High School (white) had courses such as television and advanced electronics and Austin High School (black) had courses such as brick masonry and tailoring. Course offerings were based on the jobs available to students who completed the course. Separate but equal?

Construction of new schools and maintenance of existing buildings were generally a struggle between communities. Decisions of whether to build new schools or renovate existing buildings always had racial and economic status overtones. The money for any construction was limited. All projects had to be approved by the Knoxville Board of Education and Knoxville City Council, both political bodies whose members were elected at large. In addition to legal segregation restrictions, the black population of Knoxville was only approximately 15 percent of the total population. This percentage figure ranged from 12 to 26 percent, depending on the source and date of the report. The point being, the black community had very little political clout.

School desegregation efforts in Tennessee began as early as 1950 in the nearby city of Clinton, Tennessee. That case (*Joheather McSwain et al. v. County Board of Education of Anderson County, Tennessee, et al.*) involved five high school students who had been denied admission to the one county high school in Anderson County, Clinton High School. All of the black high school students in Anderson County were being transported to the black Austin High School in Knoxville.

The facts in the *McSwain* case in Clinton were different from the situation in Knoxville. First, the *Brown I* decision had not yet happened, and the Tennessee constitution and laws prohibiting students from being taught in the same building were in full effect. Second, it involved only high school students.

Judge Robert L. Taylor presided over this case. He had been appointed US district judge for the Eastern District of Tennessee by

Judge Robert L. Taylor presided over both the Ward *and the* Goss *cases.* Photo of portrait courtesy of US District Court for the Eastern District of Tennessee, and artist John Woodrow Kelley.

President Harry Truman in 1949. Congress adjourned before he was confirmed, but he was reappointed and immediately confirmed in 1950. He denied the request of the plaintiffs to attend Clinton High School and dismissed the lawsuit. Judge Taylor would serve on the bench for the next thirty-five years and would be involved in all the early desegregation cases in the Eastern District of Tennessee.

The decision was appealed to the US Sixth Circuit Court of Appeals. This court ultimately mandated a reversal of the district court's decision and ordered that the final decree must wait for the outcome of the US Supreme Court's decision in *Brown et al. v. The Board of Education, Topeka, Kansas, et al.* This decision in 1954 would be the basis of Judge Taylor's decision to desegregate Clinton High School in the fall of 1956.

The *Brown v. Topeka Board of Education* decision on May 17, 1954, has been described as the most significant decision in the history of the Supreme Court. The decision invalidated the *Plessey v. Ferguson* decision of fifty-eight years earlier (1896) that proclaimed "separate but equal" did not violate the Fourteenth Amendment to the US Constitution (Equal Protection Amendment). The 1954 *Brown* decision held that "separate is inherently unequal" and, therefore, violates the Fourteenth Amendment. However, it applied only to education and placed the responsibility of dismantling, "root and branch," the dual systems to all school boards in any state having either state constitutional or statutory (de jure) segregation.

A short history lesson regarding the *Brown v. Topeka Board of Education* case is in order. The *Brown* case was really four cases involving four states: Kansas, South Carolina, Virginia, and Delaware. Kansas had voluntary segregation in the elementary grades by statute. The *Brown* case involved an elementary student. South Carolina had both constitutional and statutory segregation. In the South Carolina case, which had been tried, the decision was "yes," segregated schools were illegal but there was no remedy until they were integrated. Virginia had the same legal situation. Delaware had mandated segregation. The decision there was that the blacks could attend the white schools until the system was desegregated, but no indication was given as to what was to happen after the systems reached the desegregated state. These four cases were combined into the *Brown v. Board of Education of Topeka* case.

The case was first tried under Chief Justice Frederick M. Vinson in 1952. The court was split and did not come to a decision. Justice Vinson died. President Eisenhower then appointed Earl Warren as chief justice. The case was tried again in 1954, resulting in Chief Justice Warren delivering the *Brown I* decision.

Very soon after the *Brown I* decision, school desegregation efforts began in Knoxville. In less than sixty days, Rev. Frank Gordon requested a meeting with the board to discuss the immediate desegregation of the schools.[4] The board saw no need to reply. The *Knoxville News-Sentinel* reported on August 11, 1954, that the board chairman indicated a special meeting might be scheduled to discuss the matter.

Board minutes do not account for such a meeting ever taking place. An earlier editorial in the *Knoxville News-Sentinel* even labeled the request as "premature."[5] There were occasional newspaper accounts of desegregation efforts during the remainder of 1954, but minutes of the board indicate "business as usual," with most attention placed on a building program.

In 1955 the Supreme Court revisited the *Brown* case and issued another opinion. The 1954 decision became known as *Brown I*. The 1955 decision became *Brown II*. Later these decisions would be referred to just as the *Brown* decision.

The *Brown II* decision in 1955 seemed to refocus attention on desegregation of schools in Knoxville. This decision recognized that each system would have its own unique problems and solutions, but the court expected the requirements of the *Brown I* decision to be met "with all deliberate speed." Most of the whites in Knoxville interpreted "deliberate speed" to mean "take time and deliberate." The black community was focused on "speed"—"get on with it!" There was general opposition to school desegregation throughout the white community in Knoxville, as well as in other communities in the South.

A new superintendent, Thomas N. Johnston, took office on June 15, 1955. The next day, June 16, he called a meeting of the administrative staff to discuss the best approach to comply with the *Brown* decision. Johnston was aware of the eventual outcome and understood the public opposition to school desegregation. The meeting with the administrative staff was followed by the staff and members of the board discussing approaches to desegregating the school system.[6]

At a special meeting on August 17, 1955, the board formally resolved that it would act in good faith to implement the constitutional principles declared in the *Brown* decision. The board instructed the superintendent and his staff to develop a specific plan of action to desegregate the schools.[7] A committee was sent to Evansville, Indiana, to learn how desegregation had been successfully accomplished there. For the remainder of 1955, meetings with principals, staff, board members, and others resulted in the suggestion that a grade-a-year plan, patterned after the plan adopted by Nashville, might work in Knoxville.

Superintendent (1955–64) Thomas N. Johnston. Photo courtesy of the Knox County Museum of Education.

During the months of January and February of 1956, school personnel continued to work on other plans to desegregate the system. In March 1956, eight plans, or different combinations of plans, were presented to the board. Newspaper articles reporting on these plans included opinions in absolute opposition to desegregation as well as accusations of delay and "foot dragging."

After the *Brown* decision to expedite desegregation, Judge Taylor directed that racial segregation would be discontinued at Clinton High School. He decided that a reasonable time to implement desegregation was the fall term of August 27, 1956. Clinton High School would be the first publicly supported high school in the South to be desegregated.[8]

School personnel and students spent time during the later months of the 1955 term preparing for the desegregation of the Clinton High School student body. There was some opposition, but generally the students were prepared to be "decent and civil." However, a minority element of the community felt otherwise.

Demonstrations, with the assistance of an "outside agitator," John Kasper, became disorderly and dangerous. Crowds of outsiders overwhelmed the three-man Clinton police force. Threats on the lives of the school principal and black students resulted in the mobilization of the National Guard (six hundred strong) and a concentration of one hundred state highway patrolmen. Clinton was under martial law for two months.

A parade of hooded individuals in 125 automobiles, the bombing of a black family's home, and rock and egg throwing were just some of the destructive events. These intimidating and disturbing acts continued into 1958, when Clinton High School was damaged by a bomb.[9] Disturbances of the same nature were occurring in Nashville, Tennessee; Little Rock, Arkansas; and in other urban school settings in the South.

School boards throughout Tennessee were apprehensive and concerned regarding their responsibility to desegregate schools. In response to numerous requests for advice and direction, Tennessee Attorney General George McCanless issued an opinion letter to the Tennessee Commissioner of Education defining the state's legal responsibility in implementing the *Brown* mandate. He also gave an opinion regarding the responsibilities of local boards of education. The June 16, 1955, letter states:

> Under the Code of Tennessee the management of the public schools is solely the business of local school boards. This has been the law since the origin of the public school system in Tennessee and is the law today.

Under this state of the law it is the responsibility of each local school board to determine for itself the way in which it is going to meet the problem of desegregating the schools under its jurisdiction.

Each board must determine for itself, in light of all existing applicable circumstance (physical, fiscal, sociological, transportation problems, etc.) when, where, how, and to what degree the schools under its jurisdiction are to be desegregated. This imposes upon each board the duty of considering for itself its own course of action.

Local school boards which are sued by Negroes seeking admission to schools under their own action determining the manner in which their schools be desegregated. It will be necessary for legal counsel for defense of such suit to be provided by the county, the city, or special school district involved. While the office of the Attorney General is aware of the problems that will confront the school boards and is sympathetic with their problems, the office can do no more than advise with representatives of the boards with respect to these problems as they arise. Under the Constitution and the statutes of Tennessee, the office of the Attorney General is limited to representation of the state and of state officials with respect to state revenue and other state matters. Counties, cities, and special districts have always been required by law to provide their own legal counsel in matters affecting them, and this has not been changed because of the desegregation opinion; however, within the limits of our ability and to the extent permitted by the most favorable interpretation of the statutes defining and regulating our duties we stand ready to furnish such advice and guidance as under the circumstances we can.

While, as indicated above, the State Department of Education has no legal responsibility to determine the manner in which the segregation problem will be dealt with in each school district, there is much the Department can do by way of correlation of information and other things which will occur to you as the responsible head of that Department. As a result of conferences with you I know that you intend to have the Department of Education do all that it can within the framework of existing law to assist local school boards in the solution of their heavy and vexing problems.[10]

This letter actually laid the responsibility of implementing the *Brown* decision entirely on local school boards. Despite General McCanless's 1955 statement that desegregation was purely a "local school problem," in January 1957, the Tennessee Legislature passed the parental preference statutes permitting "voluntary segregation."

The board viewed these circumstances, the wording of the Supreme Court's "deliberate speed" language, and the attorney general of Tennessee's opinion as it proceeded to desegregate the system. The board was also mindful of its responsibility to conduct efficient, undisturbed, and continuous schooling for the students of the City of Knoxville.[11] Board members assumed the position that they were more reliably informed than the bearers of petitions and applications for desegregation by some black parents, organized groups, and local ministers. They were of the opinion that the great bulk of both blacks and whites in Knoxville did not want desegregation.

On May 14, 1956, the board issued a formal statement: "Further delay in inaugurating a plan will lessen the likelihood of unpleasant incidents which have occurred in some places where desegregation has been inaugurated."[12] Nevertheless, school personnel continued to work towards compliance with the Supreme Court's *Brown* decree.

Although the relationship of blacks and whites was considered harmonious within the context of de jure segregation, there is little doubt that a majority of the white community did not want school desegregation. The blacks did want desegregation, but the events in Clinton and the fact that the total number of blacks in Knoxville was only a small percentage of the total city population made it an uneasy situation for them. Violence in any form was to be avoided, if at all possible, in the school desegregation efforts as well as later civil rights activities.

Interviews with former students reflect the conflicting emotions of black pupils. They were proud of their schools, the teachers, and the importance that the community as a whole placed on education. However, there was the perception that they were only supplied with secondhand textbooks, instructional materials, desks, band uniforms and the like. Many considered their teachers as "the best" and held them in high esteem.

As events developed throughout the 1960s, many black teachers worked in the desegregation and civil rights efforts on a clandestine basis. There was a real fear of losing their jobs for participation in the civil rights efforts.

Some of the situations the blacks would point to as discriminatory could also be found in some white schools, depending on the economic status of the community. Schools in low socioeconomic areas of the city did not have as much instructional material, were issued some of the used books, and facilities might not receive maintenance monies that schools were allotted in more affluent neighborhoods. Like school systems all over the South, Knoxville schools were segregated by race and economics.

At the beginning of the fall term in 1956, several black parents attempted to enroll their youngsters in Staub Elementary School, Mountain View Elementary School, and East High School. They were denied admission. Five students appealed to the superintendent for admission to Rule High School. On December 20, 1956, one student went to the director of pupil personnel requesting transfer from Eastport Elementary School, a school designated for blacks, to Mountain View Elementary School. All of these students were denied admission.[13]

On January 7, 1957, a petition was filed with the court, *Dianne Ward et al. v. The Board of Education of the City of Knoxville, Tennessee, et al.* asking for immediate desegregation of the schools. The petitioners Dianne Ward, Byron Jones, Harneatha Massengill, Hughgenia Watkins, Alice Sylvia Jones, James E. Person, Florence Person, Loretta Thompson, Emma June Brazzell, Barbara Greene, and Frederick Greene, et al., claimed:

. . . the Tennessee Constitution of 1870, Art. 11, Sec.12: . . . No school established or aided under this section shall allow white and negro children to be received as scholars together in the same school . . .

and the Tennessee Code, 1955, Sections; 49-3701: Interracial Schools Prohibited. 49-3702: Teaching of mixed classes prohibited, and 49-3703: Penalty for violations:

Any person violating any of the provisions of this chapter, shall be guilty of a misdemeanor, and, upon conviction, shall be fined for each offense fifty dollar (50.00), and imprisonment not less than thirty (30) days nor more than six months. (Acts 1901, ch. 7, sec 3; Shan., sec 6888a39; Mod. Code 1932, sec 11397)

deprived them of their rights guaranteed by the Constitution and laws of the United States.[14]

The defendants were listed as: Andrew Johnson, D. A. Cooper, Edward C. Woods, Robert B. Ray, and Hoyle Campbell, as members of

Avon Williams (left) and Carl Cowan (right) were attorneys for the plaintiffs in both the Ward *and* Goss *cases.* Photo courtesy of the Beck Cultural Exchange Center.

the board; Thomas N. Johnston, superintendent; principals Gale Gardner, Margaret C. Hamilton, and Dewey Lee; and Frank Marable, supervisor of Child Personnel.

Carl Cowan, a Knoxville lawyer; Avon N. Williams and Z. Alexander Looby, Nashville lawyers; and Thurgood Marshall and Jack Greenberg, New York lawyers, represented the plaintiffs. Cowan was also serving as assistant Knox County attorney general. The Knox County White Citizens Council made an attempt to have Cowan dismissed from his position as assistant attorney general. The reason stated in a telegram to State Attorney General McCanless was: "He [Cowan] cannot best serve the interests of the citizens of Knox County and at the same time serve as a paid stooge of the National Association for the Advancement of Colored People."[15] Hal H. Clements Jr., Knox County attorney general, put an end to the attempt with the following statement: "Mr. Cowan is an assistant attorney general and he may take outside lawsuits if he wants to."[16]

This statement, however, did not stop other individuals from using Cowan's role in the lawsuit in other areas of political maneuvering. During the 1957 General Assembly session, Senators Hobart F. Atkins and E. B. Bowles showed a bit of hostility toward each other over three bills affecting their districts. One of the bills added two positions to the Knox County attorney general's office. Senator Bowles opposed it and accused Senator Atkins indirectly of trying to help Attorney General Clements to "enforce the integration of Knoxville schools." He charged that the bill was designed to free Clements's investigator, Carl Cowan, to push federal court legislation for ending school segregation in Knoxville.[17]

Carl Cowan served as counsel for the plaintiffs throughout the entire length of the lawsuit. His participation in the *Ward* case as well as the *Goss* case was a significant service to Knoxville's black community.

The board referred the complaint of *Ward v. Knoxville Board of Education*, to the city law director, John Duncan, for advice and representation. Employing a special counsel for the board came into consideration. The Nashville Board of Education had used this approach in its case, but the Knoxville board would have to get authorization from both the city law director and the city council. Such authorization would not come easily!

S. Frank Fowler Sr. (left) was attorney for the Knoxville Board of Education in both the Ward *and* Goss *cases. Sam F. Fowler Jr. (right) later assumed the major role in defending the board.* Photo courtesy of the Sam Fowler family.

On January 9, 1957, the board met in special session to discuss the *Ward* complaint. The only action recorded was: ". . . request the Law Director to represent the defendants, if special counsel was considered necessary, advisable, or desired, the law director and chairman of the board are authorized to agree upon counsel . . ."[18]

At a special meeting called on January 18, 1957, the board chairman reported on deliberations with the law director and moved that S. Frank Fowler be employed as counsel for the defendants.[19] No action was taken by the law director for several months, and in executive session on November 27, 1957, the board renewed its request that the city council approve the designation of Fowler as counsel for the defendants. Again, nothing happened.

Although not officially hired, Frank Fowler had been handling the *Ward* complaint since shortly after it was filed. He had filed an answer to the complaint on June 28, 1957. His response provides an insight into the attitude of the board, and probably that of the white community, toward school desegregation. More important, this response also became the basis for the board's actions in the later petition by Josephine Goss.

In his answer, Fowler quoted a portion of the superintendent's report of August 15, 1956:

> All the schools, white and colored, have been managed exactly alike from the start, save in this: white teachers have taught white schools, and colored teachers colored schools. The same course of study is in each; and same rules and regulations; the same pay for teachers of the same grade; and the same Board of Examiners for all Teachers.[20]

His argument went on with:

> In the present situation there will be a strong tendency for an abrupt change of practice. A considerable amount of additional cooperation can be obtained from the various elements of our community by patience. On the other hand, an unwise and too hasty attempt to carry out the order of the Supreme Court will seriously disrupt and impede the education of the pupils of Knoxville both white and Negro.[21]

The focus of the argument was simply more time to desegregate the schools. He indicated that the board had already taken steps to involve all segments of the community as well as the school system. Superintendent Johnston insisted that the system was moving forward in such a way as to protect the rights of all parties and to operate the schools "without serious and inequitable interruption."[22]

Interviews with black members of the community and plaintiffs indicate a perspective of the different realities in the white and black communities.

> My textbooks had names, underlining, school names, and notes to other students, not in Austin [High School], and they were supposed to be new textbooks. The white schools got the new books; we got the used ones.[23]

> Athletic programs and facilities were always hand-me-downs or developed by parents and/or community, and they were always

segregated—black tournaments and white tournaments. I had
some of the best athletes in the city, but we couldn't play against
their best. When we desegregated, the white schools recruited
our best and helped parents get transfers to their schools.[24]

I wanted to sit-in, attend the board meetings that had dele-
gations asking for desegregation, and anything else I could do,
but I was assured that I would lose my job if I did. So, I
stuffed envelopes, ran the mimeograph machine, and made
discreet phone calls.[25]

On December 3, 1957, Judge Taylor granted Fowler's motion for more
time to work out a desegregation plan.[26] On December 31, 1957, a special
meeting of the board was held with the only action being a motion, made
and passed, that Frank Fowler be terminated because the law director had
not asked city council to approve him as counsel for the defendants.

In the city elections of November 7, 1957, three new board
members were elected to replace three board members named in the
Ward complaint. The new members were Mary Ellen (Mrs. Gilmer)
Keith, Dr. John Burkhart, and Dr. Charles Moffett. Outgoing members
were D. A. Cooper, Andrew Johnson, and Hoyle Campbell. On
January 1, 1958, with three newly elected members sworn in, the board
called a meeting to discuss the *Ward* case, elect a temporary chairman,
hire Frank Fowler, and to meet with Mayor Jack Dance and other city
officials to iron out policies regarding some operational procedures.[27]

In a letter to Superintendent Johnston, dated January 2, 1958, Fowler
acknowledged that in conversation with the law director, the newly
approved city charter did not require council approval of his employment
as counsel for the board. The money had already been appropriated.[28]
Fowler was now the official defense attorney in the *Ward* complaint.

The question now became: Are the individual board members sued,
thereby adding the newly elected individuals to the suit, or is the board
an entity? The board took the position that each member had to be
defended individually, which was a good legal position since the plaintiffs had not filed a motion to substitute the newly elected members.
Fowler filed a motion on August 28, 1958, to dismiss on the basis that

the plaintiffs had not filed a motion to substitute. Plaintiffs' attorneys took the position that the board was a corporate body, a continuing entity, and that substitution was not necessary.

On September 19, 1958, plaintiffs filed a motion to substitute the newly elected members to the board for the outgoing members. On June 1, 1959, Judge Taylor denied the motion and dismissed the outgoing board members from the *Ward* case. The board had asked the defendants be designated "as members or Agents of the Board of Education." Judge Taylor granted this request.[29] Now the board was considered a "continuing entity."

The parents of the plaintiffs in the *Ward* case had experienced threats of losing their employment and other social discomforts and, after consultations with their attorneys, it was decided that this case should not go further. But the plaintiffs would only agree to the case being dismissed "without prejudice" and with the expressed right to open the same complaints at a later date. *Ward v. Knoxville Board of Education* was dismissed on June 1, 1959.

Desegregation efforts did not stop with this case. On December 11, 1959, *Josephine Goss v. Knoxville Board of Education* was filed. Fifteen years of litigation and school desegregation activities followed.

1959 Board of Education (from left to right, seated): Mary Ellen Keith, E. C. Woods, Robert Ray, John H. Burkhart, and Charles Moffett; (standing): A. C. Hutson Jr., business manager, and T. N. Johnston, superintendent. Photo courtesy of the Knox County Museum of Education.

CHAPTER 2

1960—THE BEGINNING

T HE *JOSEPHINE GOSS V. KNOXVILLE* Board of Education complaint was filed on December 11, 1959, in the US District Court for the Eastern District of Tennessee, Judge Robert L. Taylor presiding. The plaintiffs were seventeen children attending the Knoxville City Schools: Josephine Goss, Thomas A. Goss, Thomas L. Moore Jr., Theotis Robinson Jr., Dianne Ward, Donna Graves, Phyllis Roberts, Albert J. Winton Jr., Regena Arnett, Michael Arnett, Elizabeth Pearl Barber, Sharon Smith, Annie Brown, Charles Edmond McAfee, Ivan Maurice Blake, Herbert Thompson, and Eddie Riddle.

The attorneys for the plaintiffs were the same five who had represented the plaintiffs in the *Ward* case: Carl Cowan, Avon N. Williams, Z. Alexander Looby, Thurgood Marshall, and Jack Greenberg.

The defendants were members of the board: Dr. John H. Burkhart, Robert B. Ray, Edward C. Woods, Dr. Charles R. Moffett, and Mary Ellen (Mrs. Gilmer H.) Keith; Superintendent Thomas N. Johnston, R. Frank Marable, supervisor of child personnel department; assistant and acting principal Buford A. Bible; and principals L. Gale Gardner, Robert H. Cardwell, Donald E. Blackstock, and William M. Davis. (See appendix A.)

The complaint alleged that the Knoxville school system was segregated and asked for an injunction to immediately stop the operation of a segregated system. A hearing was scheduled for February 8, 1960. At this time, the plaintiffs were better organized for the struggle ahead than the defendants.

The board referred the complaint to the new city law director, T. Mack Blackburn, for advice and defense. As early as January 3, 1960, the *Knoxville News-Sentinel* published the following: "Mr. Blackburn offered to handle the lawsuit through his office or to approve retaining outside counsel, if the board desired." Dr. Burkhart, chairman of the board, said: "We decided to let his office handle it." John J. Duncan, newly elected mayor, had announced a week before that C. R. McClain, a former law director, would be retained to handle the case.

There seemed to be a problem between what the board was thinking regarding strategy and McClain's position. A newspaper article reported McClain as saying: "The board has only two choices: one to fight the complaint all the way to the Supreme Court, and probably lose, or secondly, file a desegregation plan."[1] The board still did not have a designated attorney to defend them.

Mayor John J. Duncan and other city officials were very conservative, true to their beliefs, and they, as well as the board, accurately represented the community that elected them. "These times they are a'changing," really described the climate the board would now face.

The board and the Knox County School Board met on January 8, 1960, to discuss problems arising from the city's annexation of a large area outside the present city boundaries. After this meeting, the board went into executive session and discussed the *Goss* complaint, but, according to Dr. John Burkhart, "took no action." However, in an article entitled "Lawyer In Integration Suit Hired Secretly," the *Knoxville Journal* quoted Dr. Burkhart: ". . . the board had decided to ask the mayor to hire S. Frank Fowler at the January 8, 1960, meeting and that four members of city council had agreed to put money in the 1960 budget for Mr. Fowler's fee."[2] Details of employment were finalized and "he was hired [for the *Goss* case] January 1960."[3] Fowler represented the board at the February hearing.

The restraining order and arguments were heard on February 8, 1960. Fowler began: "I have my orders . . . the board has stated they don't intend to present a plan unless ordered." Judge Taylor's impatience began to show as he snapped back: "You tell them they are not writing this court's orders." Fowler, as he argued for more time to prepare a plan, referred once or twice to the violence that Clinton, Tennessee, had experienced after being ordered to desegregate schools. "I have been long-suffering with you this morning," Judge Taylor told Fowler, and was very emphatic with the remark: "They'd better get a plan in here by April 8 or we will see what happens."[4]

Avon Williams, plaintiffs' attorney, indicated that their witnesses were in court and ready to argue the restraining order request. Nevertheless, Judge Taylor said there was no need to act on the request until the board had submitted a plan.[5] The hearing was adjourned until April 8, 1960.

There are no entries in the docket until the April 8 continued session for hearing the request for the restraining order and the presentation of the plan of desegregation by the board. The board had a difficult time coming to agreement on a plan. Eight different plans had been developed and discussed for months. Judge Taylor had given an indication that since the Nashville "grade-a-year" plan had been approved by the court, he might look favorably on such a plan for Knoxville.

As the board floundered with producing a plan that members could support or even discuss, a newspaper account described a problem that had developed. According to the newspaper "secret" meetings or executive sessions had been held where decisions were made and reported to the media as "board decisions." Some members claimed to be unaware of the alleged actions. Board member Robert Ray was quoted: "We have no plan that I know . . ."[6] Dr. John H. Burkhart, board chairman, had said earlier that the board would come up with a "Knoxville plan," but other board members at that time indicated such a plan had not been discussed with them.[7]

The board set March 30, 1960, for a meeting to adopt a plan. The meeting was an emotional one filled with speeches, insinuations, name-calling, a false fire alarm, and the change of a long-standing board policy regarding personal privilege. Superintendent Johnston presented the grade-a-year plan. It was one of nine plans that had been developed, and was simply referred to as "Plan Nine" during the discussion. Johnston detailed elements of the plan and pointed out that similar plans had been adopted in several systems. Since Nashville had developed such a plan that was approved by the court, he was of the opinion that Judge Taylor would look favorably on this plan.

Audience at the Knoxville Board of Education meeting at the adoption of the grade-a-year plan, 1960. Photo courtesy of the *Knoxville News-Sentinel.*

A motion was made to adopt the plan but died for lack of a second. Board member Ray asked if anyone favored the plan. He said: "I'm against it. The Fellowship House [a local pro-integration organization] is against it and the NAACP is against it."[8] This seemed a pretty safe statement since the NAACP was against anything other than immediate and total desegregation.

Attorney Fowler, understanding the mandate of the court, told the board: "You must produce a plan. You are the elected administrators of these schools and must meet the problems that occur while you are in office. You ask if anyone favors this plan. Regardless of how I feel, I know a plan has to be adopted. Therefore, I favor this plan. It has been tested in a sister city. I am not going to sit silently and leave the impression that the plan has no supporters." Ray then asked: "What would you do if we decide not to support a plan?" Fowler indicated that he would go back to court and "tell it so."[9]

After a short recess, one of three, the chair asked to hear from members of the audience. Several members presented their views of the plan or on desegregation in general. Lewis Sinclair, vice president of the Knoxville Area Human Relations Council, presented some "principles" calling for complete desegregation of schools. Rev. R. E. James, pastor of Mt. Zion Baptist Church, indicated he thought the plan had "disadvantages" and listed undue length of time; children from the same family would have to attend different schools; black students would be denied vocational courses; all black children now in school would be denied the opportunity "to realize their full potential for a creative life in freedom and dignity;" and other items of concern. A member of the audience, a retired vaudeville actor, said: "The Negro had better wake up. He is being used as a tool." A Mr. H. H. Hall spoke in favor of a speedier plan.[10]

Fowler renewed his plea to adopt a plan. He argued that the board was better able to develop a plan, as they had some skills in school matters, rather than a judge whose skills were mainly in the realm of law.[11] The board still could not agree, but after the last of the recesses, a motion was made to reconvene at a "later date" for the board to "make its plans as to what it will do on April 8th."[12] Time was running out. Anger, desperation, and frustration would bring on a lot of "behind the scene" activity over the next week.

The board held a special session on April 4, 1960. This meeting had a completely different atmosphere than prior meetings. The chairman opened the meeting by leading an invocation and pledge to the flag. Board member Dr. Charles Moffett immediately presented the following statement:

> Realizing that the present Supreme Court of the United States has held unconstitutional the interpretation of the Fourteenth Amendment which was held by previous Supreme Court for many years and having been ordered by the Federal Judge of this District to submit a plan of desegregation by April 8, 1960, it becomes imperative that this Knoxville City Board of Education examine carefully what its action will be. As I recall, this Board laid some ground rules for resolving this most serious and revolutionary problem some time ago. These ground rules include the following:

1. That this Board was agreed that it *would* submit a plan of desegregation to the Federal Judge on April 8, 1960.

2. That a majority action of the Board would constitute a decision and that those members who could not agree with that particular plan would as members of the minority group accept the decision of the majority and support the plan wholeheartedly. Some members of the Board have been referred to as being the minority group. I was not aware that there existed a minority group. The Board Meeting held on Wednesday, March 30, 1960, failed to act on the plans previously submitted by the Administration even though there was admittedly a majority. This majority, when presented with the motion by Mrs. Gilmer Keith to the effect that this Board should accept the superintendent's recommendation that is Plan #9 which was presented by the superintendent at the Board meeting failed to act and the motion died for lack of a second.

The entire Board has worked long and hard on this most serious and controversial problem. Each member, so far as I am concerned, has carefully weighed the circumstances involving our local situation and has diligently attempted to arrive at the best decision. In view of the above facts, and not wishing to obstruct the most peaceful and orderly plan possible for our Knoxville Schools, I wish to submit the following motion: I move that the Board follow the recommendation of the superintendent and submit Plan #9 to the Federal Judge on April 8, 1960.[13]

Board member Roy E. Linville (who had been elected to replace Edward C. Woods) seconded the motion and made a statement regarding the board's responsibilities. The vote was taken. There were four ayes and one nay. Dr. Moffett immediately read and moved the adoption of the following resolution:

The Board of Education calls upon all people of goodwill in Knoxville to join in an attempt to comply with Court Orders and to deal effectively with the question at issue in such a manner as to reflect deserved credit upon our wonderful city. The Board is fully mindful of the fact that time is short for the orientation work required and for this reason, among others, call upon all citizens, wherever possible, to join it in its attempt to make possible for its students, teachers, super-visors, and administrative staff, the most satisfactory adjustment to this gigantic challenge. In effect, the question of desegregation in the public schools is a community-wide problem and requires complete community cooperation in arriving at a solution. Finally, it is the earnest hope of this Board that all of the people of Knoxville concerned with this problem will understand that the Board of Education will stand *firmly* back of its agents in an attempt to comply in all good faith with mandate of the law and rulings of the courts on the subject of desegregation.[14]

The motion passed unanimously.

Both the *Knoxville News-Sentinel* and the *Knoxville Journal* carried details of the meeting the next day. The headline for the *Knoxville Journal* read, "Grade-a-Year Integration Proposed by City Board."[15] The *Knoxville News-Sentinel* was a little more subdued with, "Integration of Grade-a-Year OK'd."[16] Both newspapers pointed out the fact that the vote was four to one, and gave some attention to Ray's objections. Fowler presented this plan to the court clerk on April 8, 1960. (See appendix B.)

After years of responding to the *Brown* decisions in the same fashion that most of the southern boards responded (delaying, ignoring, squabbling, etc.), the board did what had to be done. In retrospect, it is fair to say that the board went into school desegregation "kicking and screaming," but they did represent the citizens who elected them. As noted earlier, the black population in Knoxville was only approximately 15 percent and public officials were elected at large.

The plan adopted by the board and presented to the court was immediately challenged. The *Knoxville News-Sentinel* reported, "Grade-a-Year Plan Too Slow." In the same article, mention was made of some concern that the transfer provisions would perpetuate segregation. This policy provides: ". . . if a student finds himself in a school that is predominately populated by pupils of the other race, he may be transferred to some other school in his zone."[17] This section of the transfer policy would be challenged by the plaintiffs until 1963, when the Supreme Court reversed the district and appeals courts' approval.

At the hearing on August 8, 1960, Carl Cowan opened his argument with an attack on the "good faith" of the board. "They sat on their hands for five years without adopting a plan and the plan presented is the Nashville plan word for word." Further, ". . . none of the plaintiffs in the suit will ever be able to attend a desegregated school."[18]

Fowler countered: ". . . the proof we will present will overcome all these objections." He then laid the foundation for his philosophy for the case. He admitted that the system was segregated and had operated on a segregated basis for generations; that desegregation was not sought nor desired by the vast majority of the Knoxville community; that segregation had adverse effects on students; that there had existed racially discriminatory practices; and that the board had not started desegregation, even though it had been five years since the *Brown* decision.

The board justified its position insofar as the "duties of the defendants have sharply clashed; the one to obey the Constitution of the United States as so recently interpreted; the second to honor and respect an allegiance to our community and its members which incorporates in its very fabric a careful protection of our cherished institutions."[19] Whether the board used the word "institutions" to mean education or segregation was not plain. The plaintiffs interpreted it as the latter.

Those complaints having to do with the practice and detrimental effects of segregation were admitted and effectively "off the table." The case from the very beginning would be about "the plan." Testimony and argument regarding why the board chose the "grade-a-year" plan was presented. The merits of going slow with integration of schools and the difficulties of managing an integrated system were presented by Superintendent Johnston and members of the board and staff.

After three days of trial, Judge Taylor told the attorneys that he would not go through the entire voluminous record in the case but would "decide it on what I hear."[20] He had previously indicated that he would have an early decision, and he was true to his word. On August 19, 1960, Judge Taylor approved the plan for desegregating the Knoxville schools as submitted by the board, with one exception: the provision relating to the vocational and technical program at Fulton High School.

The board was "directed to restudy the problem presented with reference to the technical and vocational courses offered in the Fulton High School, to which colored students who desire these technical and vocational courses [have] an opportunity to take them."[21] The vocational program and the transfer policies would turn out to be very difficult problems.

Judge Taylor had given the plaintiffs ten days from the filing of the plan to file objections. The plaintiffs objected on several grounds, the main concern being: " . . . that [the plan] did not provide for elimination of racial segregation as required by the Due Process and Equal Protection Clause of the Fourteenth Amendment to the Constitution of the United States."[22]

Rev. Carrol M. Felton accompanying a student who was enrolling in the first grade in 1960. Photo courtesy of the *Knoxville News-Sentinel.*

First grade registration, 1960.
Photo courtesy of the *Knoxville News–Sentinel.*

The board held a special meeting on August 22, 1960, to react to the order of the court. It adopted new zone lines for the schools which were involved with first grade. These schools had single boundaries. All the other schools had dual zone lines because all grades above the first grade were still segregated. The superintendent was instructed to immediately start a study of the vocational programs at Fulton and Austin to comply with the court's request. Of major concern was the vocational transfer policy included as a part of the desegregation plan.

A plan to provide vocational and technical training for black students *similar* to those offered for white students at Fulton High School was filed with the court on March 31, 1961. The plan was extensive and detailed. Major elements were:

1. Continued vocational and technical courses at both Fulton and Austin High Schools.
2. Provided unimpeded transfers where course is provided at only one school.
3. Maintained the present courses and establishes new courses when fifteen or more students want them, whether they be white or black or mixed.
4. Set up criteria for the establishment of new courses, which criteria are not related to race.
5. Expressly forbade racial discrimination.

The plaintiffs filed objections to the plan on April 10, 1961. These objections were:

1. The plan does not eliminate segregation in vocational and technical training.
2. This plan fails to take into account the delay of nearly seven years which has occurred since the *Brown* decision.
3. Paragraph four (new courses criteria), is an attempt to justify delay that does not meet the enumerated reasons set out by the Supreme Court.
4. Standards are vague with respect to how a student is to be regarded as a qualified applicant for technical training, and that this vagueness may result in racial discrimination.
5. The provisions of the plan will only apply to Negro children in the future.[23]

The board filed a memorandum dealing with the objections on June 14, 1961. The defendants' answers to objections were:

1. Clearly the plan does eliminate such segregation.
2. The plan is fully effective immediately, and the objection is completely without substance.
3. The plan is broadly phrased and contains no language, in standards or elsewhere, whatever having the limiting effect which plaintiffs claim results from the language of the plan; furthermore, the plan expressly forbids racial discrimination.
4. The plan applies to white children as well as Negro children in the future.
5. It is respectfully submitted that each and every one of the objections of the plaintiffs should be overruled as being without substance, and the plan should be approved and put into operation in the school year beginning September 1961.[24]

These court proceedings were amid problems with summer schools. The grade-a-year had just started and the board was not thinking about desegregating any program, other than parts of the vocational programs, above the first grade. The black community had other thoughts. The

Knoxville News-Sentinel carried an article on June 6, 1961, captioned, "Ministers Interfere, Negro Summer School Principal Charges."

At the regular board meeting in June 1961, Dewey Roberts, principal of Green Elementary School and principal-to-be of the summer school, reported that three ministers were present at registration for the Austin summer school and discouraged students from registering or offered to take them to Catholic High to register.

The three ministers—Rev. Matthew A. Jones Sr., president of the Knoxville branch of the National Association for the Advancement of Colored People (NAACP); Rev. Frank Gordon, chairman of the NAACP education committee; and Rev. R. E. James, head of the Associated Council for Full Citizenship—were present at the June board meeting. Each spoke regarding the upcoming summer school session.

Rev. Frank Gordon was an early advocate for school desegregation. He appeared before the Knoxville Board of Education and petitioned for complete desegregation of the system less than sixty days after the Brown *decision in 1954.*
Photo courtesy of the Beck Cultural Exchange Center.

Reverend Gordon asked the board to develop a policy to the effect that if a child couldn't get a course he wanted at one summer school he could enroll in the other. (There was a summer school for white students at West High School.) He added: "You know how expensive a lawsuit is." He was referring to the *Goss* case which had resulted in the grade-a-year plan the summer before. Reverend James gave the board very little credit for desegregation efforts by saying: "Segregation in summer school is just as distasteful as the segregation we already have."[25]

Dr. John Burkhart responded with a reminder that the board did not initiate the lawsuit, that the board was operating under a court order of gradual desegregation, that he had heard of coercion that might cause the board to abandon the plans for the summer school, and that the board had submitted a plan to desegregate the vocational programs. He ended his remarks with: "We're not dragging our feet. The summer schools should not be desegregated."[26]

The ministers denied having interfered with the registration process, but did remark: "If we can't desegregate the Negro schools, we'll integrate the Catholics."[27]

The *Knoxville News-Sentinel* reported that the superintendent had ordered the Austin summer school closed. Only about thirty students showed up for the opening day of summer classes, even though over one hundred had been expected. Superintendent Johnston said the number of pickets increased to "about 35 ministers, students, and older people." Roberts, the appointed summer school principal, remarked: "It was a sacrifice move they wanted the children to make."[28]

On June 19, 1961, Judge Taylor issued a memorandum opinion in which he said that the board "has made a good faith effort to submit a supplemental plan that meets the requirements of the Constitution and that deals justly with the school children of Knoxville . . . [29] There was, however, one reservation that Judge Taylor illustrated in this manner: "A student who lives near Fulton and who possesses the necessary vocational qualifications to enter Fulton should not be required to travel across town to attend Austin when Fulton is much nearer."[30] The court "requested" the superintendent and board ". . . to restudy this one phase of the problem and try to present a plan that will meet the difficulty if it is a real difficulty . . ."[31]

Judge Taylor added another sentence that illustrated the attitude of the court and provided both parties with an idea as to how far the judge would go into the management of the school system. He stated: "The Board of Education is charged with the responsibility of operating Fulton and Austin High Schools, and this Court will not interfere except where necessary to protect Constitutional rights."[32]

Judge Taylor never wavered from holding the board accountable for not violating the constitutional rights of students and parents, and for managing a plan of desegregation, but he never injected the court into the day-to-day operations of the school system.

On July 14, 1961, a statement was filed on behalf of the board in response to the court's opinion of June 19, 1961. The statement said in part: ". . . the Fulton plan as amended and approved by the court, if changed so as to carry out the suggestion of the court, would cause serious trouble . . ." The trouble the board was referring to had to do with building capacity at Fulton and the effect on the Austin program caused by diminished student numbers.

Plaintiffs filed objections to the board's statement on July 27, 1961, and a motion for modification of the court's judgment of June 19, 1961. The motion was heard on September 14, 1961, and overruled.

The board was beginning to hear complaints from Vine Junior High School, Park City Lowry Elementary, and Austin High School regarding the inadequacies of the facilities. At the regular meeting on September 11, 1961, Rev. Frank Gordon appeared in the interest of Eddie Davis, a student who wanted to take a class at Fulton High School that was at capacity. On October 16, 1961, Rev. Matthew A. Jones Sr., spokesman for a Park City group, called the board's attention to overcrowded classrooms, no facilities for speech and Spanish classes, and the need for a special education classroom.

B. A. Ward, representing the Vine Junior High School PTA, asked for additional classrooms to accommodate the increasing enrollment as well as bleachers for the gym. At that same meeting, the superintendent reported to the board that the staff was looking into the overcrowding situation at Austin High School.

Judge Taylor issued a memorandum opinion on September 20, 1961. He approved the vocational plan as amended and ordered the board to put it into effect. The case was taken off the docket. The plaintiffs immediately filed an appeal, and on October 11, 1961, the complete record was mailed to the US Sixth Circuit Court of Appeals, Cincinnati, Ohio.[33]

CHAPTER 3

1962 TO 1964—THE PLAN

A S THE CASE WAITED TO GET ON THE docket of the US Sixth Circuit Court of Appeals, there were other Tennessee cases on appeal that would directly affect efforts in Knoxville. And there were court decisions in cases outside Tennessee that would do the same. In a letter to Superintendent Thomas Johnston dated March 12, 1962, Frank Fowler called attention to the fact that the Sixth Circuit Court of Appeals had appeals from three of the Tennessee cases. He mentioned that US District Judge W. Frank Wilson had just recently approved the grade-a-year plan for Chattanooga, but that the decision would probably be appealed also.

Fowler then speculated as to how the Sixth Circuit Court of Appeals might operate in the future. "It may be that the Court of Appeals will wait until the Chattanooga case is appealed also and argued up there in Cincinnati. Or, the Court may proceed to dispose of the three cases it now has. The Court might conceivably come with some plan to fit the whole state, in which case one would anticipate that we would all be speeded up to get abreast of the Nashville schools."[1]

The Sixth Circuit Court of Appeals had affirmed the Nashville plan that the District Court for the Middle District of Tennessee had approved. As of September 1962, Nashville's grade-a-year plan desegregated grades one through five. The similarities between the Knoxville plan and that of Nashville, particularly as it pertained to transfers, was significant. Both plans contained "freedom of choice" transfers that would become an issue in the very near future.[2]

The desegregation cases being decided during this period (1960–70), of which the Sixth Circuit Court of Appeals would consider relevant to the desegregation plan of Knoxville and other plans in the Sixth Circuit should be summarized at this point. The main decisions, but not all, were: *Swann v. Charlotte-Mecklenburg*, 402 U.S., which required busing to fulfill the mandate of *Brown I*; *Alexander v. Board of Education*, 396 U.S. 19 (1969), which had to do with attendance zone lines; and *Norcross v. Board of Education*, 397 U.S. 19, 20, 90 S.Ct. 29, 30, 24 L.Ed. 2nd 246 (1970), which required faculty desegregation.

The attorneys in the *Goss* case were notified on April 18, 1962, that the Sixth Circuit Court of Appeals: ". . . has granted the motion of appellants to advance this case for hearing and it will be set for argument at the June session of the court. The session will convene on Monday, May 28, 1962, and will continue through Saturday, June 9, 1962."[3]

The appeal was argued on May 28, 1962. The next day, Fowler sent a letter to Johnston. In part, it read:

> I have just returned from Cincinnati after argument of this case as to the Fulton Plan part of it. The position of the Board of Education which I discussed with you and Mr. Aslinger [director of Vocational and Technical Education] on May 25 was fully explained to the Court, as well as additional legal aspects of the case in the light of cases deemed pertinent, as well as in the light of its own decision on the first part of this case, which I myself deem controlling on the Fulton aspect, insofar as unconstitutionality of denial of access to the white school and also as to provision of merely equal educational instruction.

> Let me emphasize that the Court particularly inquired as to the Board's progress in acceleration of the grade-a-year plan. They made it plain that this must be effective at the beginning of the term next fall.[4]

On June 8, 1962, the Sixth Circuit Court of Appeals issued a deci-sion affirming the district court's approval of the Knoxville plan in part, modifying in part, and remanding the cause for further proceedings.

The court rejected the plan for the Fulton High School vocational and technical program and ordered the board to submit to the district court a plan that would allow black students to take advantage of the special courses at that school. It also denied injunctive relief, but did express the opinion ". . . that more grades than contemplated by the board's plan should now be desegregated. In the light of the board's experience with present plan, it should be enabled to submit an amended plan that will accelerate desegregation and more nearly comply with the mandate of the Supreme Court for 'good faith compliance at the earliest practicable date.'"[5]

The board now had marching orders. The grade-a-year plan was becoming questionable with the court of appeals as well as the transfer provisions for vocational students and transfers between schools for all students. After receiving notice from the clerk of the district court in Knoxville, Fowler wrote a letter to Dr. John Burkhart, chairman of the board, on June 11, 1962, to the effect that the Sixth Circuit Court of Appeals had directed the board to speed up the desegregation schedule. He further stated: "It is obvious that the Court expects compliance and they expressly stated that they expect this to be done in the term begin-ning in September 1962."[6]

The plaintiffs filed a Notice for Further Relief on June 18, 1962, requesting the court ". . . to require the defendants to file immediately, a supplemental plan for accelerating desegregation of the City Schools of Knoxville, Tennessee as of the beginning of the 1962–1963 academic school year."[7]

Fowler filed a response to the Notice for Further Relief on June 22, 1962, saying: ". . . defendants say that the pressure of problems of annexation and the proposal to consolidate the city and county school systems has delayed completion of an amended plan of desegregation, and may further delay this, but defendants expect to file such a plan by August 1 of this year."[8]

At a special meeting of the board on June 25, 1962, Superintendent Johnston recommended that the desegregation schedule be accelerated to include the third and fourth grades effective September 1, 1962. The board approved the superintendent's recommendation, and Fowler filed the amendment with the court on August 15, 1962.

The *Knoxville News-Sentinel* reported on September 8, 1962: "Negroes Seek Fast Mixing." The article said the blacks wanted more grades than the fourth desegregated and complained that the plan did not take into account the amount of time already passed since the *Brown* decision.

The annexation of a large portion of the suburbs around Knoxville in 1963 tripled the size of the city from twenty-one to seventy-seven square miles. This action added eighteen schools to the Knoxville school system. On a household basis, between 1960 and 1970, Knoxville's black community was reduced from 16.7 percent to 11.8 percent of the total city population.

In addition to the number of students added to the Knoxville system, most of them white, the grade organization of the Knox County schools was of a different pattern than the grade organization of the Knoxville schools. County schools had what was referred to as an "eight/four" system by which grades one through eight were housed in the elementary school facilities and grades nine through twelve were in high school facilities.

The city school used a "six/three/three" grade organization plan. The elementary facilities housed grades one through six; grades seven through nine were housed in junior high facilities; and grades ten through twelve were housed in high school facilities. These organizational patterns were generally the rule in each system, but there were exceptions in both because of building capacity or enrollment decreases.

Such organization patterns required different curriculum delivery systems, different programs, different textbooks, and different management of extra curricular activities. The county schools were not located as community schools. Distances between home and school had forced the county to have a transportation system for many years. The annexation agreement provided that the county would continue transportation for those students and schools annexed, but did not allow for transportation to any of the other schools in the city.

All of these concerns would have an impact on the board's actions, as well as those of the plaintiffs, over the remainder of the life of the case. The transfer policy in its entirety did not give the board's attorney much worry, but paragraph six of the policy did give him concern. Paragraph six read as follows:

> The following will be regarded as some of the valid conditions to support requests for transfer:
> a. When a white student would otherwise be required to attend a school previously serving colored students only;
> b. When a colored student would otherwise be required to attend a school previously serving white students only;
> c. When a student would otherwise be required to attend a school where the majority of students of that school or in his grade are of a different race.[9]

On August 3, 1962, the Sixth Circuit Court of Appeals affirmed the plan approved by the district court, insofar as it pertained to the grades already desegregated; designation of attendance zones based on location and capacity of buildings; and the permission for students to attend schools designated for their zones. The transfer policy was approved on the condition that it not be used to perpetuate segregation.

On August 15, 1962, the board presented the court with an amendment to the desegregation plan to include the fourth grade as well as the third grade in the grade-a-year desegregation schedule.[10] This amendment accelerated the desegregation schedule by a year. Grades one through four and the vocational programs at Austin and Fulton High Schools would be desegregated by September 1, 1962. Two years after the beginning of the grade-a-year plan started, four grades were already desegregated.

Plaintiffs filed Specifications of Objections to the amended plan on September 18, 1962, and amended it further the next day. These objections, in summary, were:

1. The amended plan did not provide for the elimination of racial segregation of the Knoxville schools "with all deliberate speed."
2. The plan did not take into account the period of over five years which elapsed during which the board completely failed and refused to comply with the said requirements of the due process clauses of the Fourteenth Amendment and prior court decisions.
3. The plan does not take into account the period of over eight years which have elapsed since the first *Brown* decision.
4. The additional eight year period required by the plan is not "necessary in the public interest" and is not "consistent with good faith compliance at the earliest practicable date."
5. The board has not carried their burden of showing any problems related to school administration arising from the physical condition of the school plant, the transportation system, personnel, revision of attendance zones, and revision of local laws and regulations which may be necessary in solving the problems.
6. The amended plan forever deprives the plaintiffs and all other Negro children now enrolled in school above the fourth grade of their rights to a racially unsegregated public education, except for the vocational courses at Fulton and Austin High Schools.
7. The plan does not allow Negro students to attend a summer school in the attendance zone of residence.[11]

The board replied to the Specifications of Objections on October 16, 1962. The reply was short and to the point. It was as follows:

> The amended plan, to which the objections are addressed, present a good faith determination by the defendant Board of Education in expediting the desegregation process in the public schools of Knoxville, Tennessee, in full compliance with the decision on this case of the United States Court of Appeals for the Sixth Circuit.
>
> The objections merely seek a reconsideration of factual matters which were fully and deliberately explored and

considered in the various hearings that have already taken place in this case and in this Court. Some of the objections specified are simply copied from objections previously filed to the plan originally submitted. There is no reason why this case should be retried upon facts found to be true by this Court and accepted by the Court of Appeals.

The defendant Board of Education in good faith has determined the full extent to which the mandate of the Court of Appeals, directing speedier desegregation, can be carried out under the circumstances of this community. It appears inequitable that the defendant should be subjected to the harassment of repeated petitions to this court.[12]

At a regular meeting of the board in December 1962, Superintendent Johnston discussed a letter from Fowler stating that the plaintiffs had filed objections to the board's plan to speed up desegregation and that the Supreme Court was reviewing the transfer provisions and that it would be argued early in 1963. He also indicated that the amendments to the plan would not keep the court from wanting "to know precisely what part race will play in the board's transfer policy in the future." He further stated: "The decision in our case will have wide application in other sections of the South."[13]

Attorneys from other systems outside of Tennessee were inquiring about the status and progress of the *Goss* case. Many expressed the desire to enter the case as amicus curiae (friend of the court). The *Knoxville News-Sentinel* carried an article stating that the Charlottesville, Virginia, school system had its plan denied by the US District Court in Richmond, Virginia, and had appealed to the US Court of Appeals. The Charlottesville appeal mentioned the fact that other circuit courts had given different decisions in similar cases and asked that the Charlottesville case be included in the Knoxville case because of the similarities.[14]

Davidson County, Tennessee, was already included in the appeal. Memphis and Chattanooga wanted in, and the attorneys for Knoxville and Nashville had agreed to accept them but would not be cooperative in the efforts of others to join.[15] All concerned knew that it did not make any difference if they cooperated or not. These parties had no control over the court's power to permit others to join.

In executive session on March 11, 1963, Fowler urged the board to take action on accelerating the desegregation schedule as requested by the court. His urging was described by one board member as being "rather direct."[16]

No other events are evidenced by the docket until March 16, 1963. However, the board had been actively amending the desegregation plan to conform to the mandates of the court, dealing with the problems with pending annexation, and with an effort to consolidate the city and county school systems.

On March 16 the board filed with the court a certified copy of a resolution passed on March 11, 1963, and it was accompanied by a report to the court on the desegregation activities of the board. It had also been decided to include the fifth and sixth grades in the desegregation schedule for the fall of 1963 and to desegregate the distributive education and Van Gilder Occupational Training Center.[17]

Josephine Goss as a sixteen-year-old student at Austin High School, plaintiff in the Josephine Goss, et al. v. Knoxville Board of Education *case.* Photo courtesy of Josephine Goss Sims.

Plaintiffs filed objections to the board's resolution and amended plan of desegregation report on March 28, 1963. These objections were:

The plaintiffs, Josephine Goss et al. respectfully object to the second Amended plan filed in the above entitled cause on or about the 15th day of March 1963 by the defendant, the Board of Education of the City of Knoxville, Tennessee; and applicable prayers thereto filed by the said Plaintiffs on September 18, 1962, and, therefore, pray that the same be incorporated herein by reference, except that Prayer No. 3 be modified to the extent that said supplemental and realistic plan to be effective not later than the beginning of the Summer Term of the City Schools of Knoxville in June 1963. Plaintiffs further pray that the Court hear this matter together along with the Amended Plan of the defendant, and plaintiffs' objections thereto, which have been docketed for a hearing on the 1st day of April, 1963.[18]

Those objections referred to as being filed in September of 1962, six months earlier, would show up several times over the next few years. The objections always centered on the plan being too slow, not inclusive enough, and that some all-black schools and some all-white schools still existed. This is a good example of the different interpretations of "all deliberate speed." To some, mostly the white community, it meant "go slow, be deliberate." To others, it meant "speed it up." The Supreme Court's decision to use the word combination of "deliberate" and "speed" has been discussed by many legal scholars. This unusual combination of words almost never, if ever, appeared in earlier court decisions.

Early objections to the Knoxville plan were concerned with the availability of vocational programs. Before the 1964 Civil Rights Act, some jobs were not available to blacks. The school system had taken the position over the years that encouraging or allowing a student to take a vocational course in an area in which they could not get employment was a waste of the student's time and the system's money. But after the appeals court decision, that was not a consideration.

The plaintiffs' Appeal Petition for Certiorari (regarding transfers) to the US Supreme Court was granted and heard on March 20–21, 1963, along with the Davidson County case involving a similar question. The Department of Justice joined the case as amicus curiae opposing the transfer plan. Attorney Fowler argued the case, describing the Knoxville desegregation plan as a "quietly conducted project" and "the Knoxville School Board is proud of its unpublicized achievements."[19]

Attorney Jack Greenberg argued the case for the NAACP. He referred to the transfer plan as ". . . the school board enforcement of private prejudice and perpetuates segregation." After hearing from US Assistant Attorney General Burke Marshall, who asked that the plan be stricken; attorney Harlan Dodson, representing Davidson County; and attorney Jack Petree, representing the Memphis School Board, the Supreme Court took the case under advisement.[20] The *Knoxville News-Sentinel* reported on June 2, 1963: "Pupil Transfers in Danger, Justice Department and NAACP Against."

The Supreme Court gave its decision on June 3, 1963. The transfer policies were held invalid because they "promoted segregation."[21] The decision was reported the same day in the *Knoxville News-Sentinel*: "School Transfer System Barred. Knox/Davidson Plan Ruled Out."

On August 14, 1963, a certified copy of the order of the Supreme Court of the United States reversing judgment (April 3, 1962, district court) remanded the case to the Sixth Circuit Court of Appeals with instructions to remand the case to district court; and further ordered that petitioners Josephine Goss et al. recover $1,542.65 for costs expended. This was the only reimbursement for costs or attorney fees granted by the courts during the entire history of the case.

The same day, August 14, 1963, a certified copy of the order of the Sixth Circuit Court of Appeals was filed, vacating the order entered on April 3, 1962, insofar as the approval of the transfer system; and further insofar as the judgment approving the transfer system "is reversed."[22]

On April 1, 1963, at a special meeting in attorney Fowler's office, the board decided to desegregate summer school at both Tyson Junior and West High effective June 1963.

On April 1–4, 1963, a hearing in the district court on the Specifications of Objections to the amended plan was held. Fowler presented the desegregation plan with all the amendments to date and presented testimony to support it. Attorney Avon Williams vigorously presented arguments for the objections to the plan.

The court approved the desegregation plan through the sixth grade, ordered that distributive education be made available to blacks, either in white or black schools, and ordered the Van Gilder program be desegregated in its present location or a similar program be established at Austin High School. Further, the court ordered that all summer schools would be desegregated. The plan and all amendments were to be effective with the beginning of the 1963 summer school session.

The board was ordered to establish a plan regarding the Fulton vocational program that would fully conform to the opinion of the Sixth Circuit Court of Appeals, as announced on July 6, 1962. The court retained jurisdiction during the period of transition.[23]

Judge Taylor's opinion approving the amendments to the desegregation plan was filed on April 29, 1963. The plaintiffs appealed this decision and filed Specifications of Objections on May 2, 1963.

The role that the board's counsel, Frank Fowler, played in keeping the plan on track is illustrated by a letter he wrote to the superintendent on May 7, 1963:

> Dear Tom,
>
> I want to call your attention to the fact that the order entered by the Federal District Judge on April 4, 1963 in this case said that at or before May 15, 1963 the Board of Education must take further action and immediately report it to the Court relative to, first, change in administration and transfers procedure in the Fulton plan and so make the plan conform to the opinion of the Court of Appeals; second, enlarge the Van Gilder program so as to provide equal and like courses of training at Austin, or if not there provided, then the Negroes be given the benefit of this program elsewhere; third, similar action in the distributive education courses.
>
> The plaintiffs in this case are in the process of making up a record for the Court of Appeals. I urge that you give this matter of complying with the Court's order full priority so that it will be done before May 15, which is only a week off.[24]

On May 15, 1963, the board reported to the district court the changes made in the desegregation plan to comply with the April 4 mandate of the court. These changes were:

1. FULTON HIGH SCHOOL TRANSFER PLAN.
   Amend the present transfer policy between Austin High
   School and Fulton High School to read as follows:

   All students enrolling in any vocational course are required by
   state authorities to meet the qualifications set out in the State
   Plan for Vocational Training.

   Qualified students desiring vocational training not offered in
   their own school may transfer to Fulton High School or to
   Austin High School to obtain such training without regard to
   race. Qualified students will be accepted in the order in which
   they apply without regard to race.

   Transfers will be expedited without regard to race through the
   Child Personnel and Attendance Department following the
   usual accounting procedures which are followed in all transfers
   between city schools. The following procedure is required:
   a. Application for transfer will be made prior to the end of
      the school year preceding the actual transfer so that
      contractual or guardian arrangements can be made with
      the State Department of Vocational Education before the
      next term begins.
   b. For accounting purposes, three copies of the transfer
      request shall be filled out and signed by the applying
      student and one of which shall also be signed by the parent.
   c. The Child Personnel Office shall supply the receiving
      school with the record of the student and the transfer
      notice as soon as possible after the close of the school year.

2. VAN GILDER OCCUPATIONAL TRAINING
   CENTER.
   Expand the Van Gilder Occupational Training Program to
   provide for additional qualified students without regard to
   race, effective September 1963.

3. DISTRIBUTIVE EDUCATION.
    Establish a Distributive Education Program at Austin High
    School effective September 1963.[25]

The plaintiffs appealed, and a certified record on appeal was mailed to the US Court of Appeals, Sixth Circuit, Cincinnati, Ohio, on June 7, 1963.

In 1964 administration of the school system gained an additional set of guidelines regarding desegregation as the result of the passage of the 1964 Civil Rights Act. The courts had not yet defined what a "unitary" system looked like, how it operated, or what it "was." The board had to operate according to the plan approved/ordered by the court, the regulations frequently coming from the US Office of Civil Rights; US Office of Health, Education, and Welfare (HEW); and the Tennessee Department of Education. The changes that were needed had become even more amplified.

Knoxville citizens were aware of problems other cities were having with school desegregation. The Ku Klux Klan burned crosses and demonstrated in Louisiana as systems attempted to desegregate public and parochial schools.[26] Mississippi was embroiled in the James Meredith attempt to enter the University of Mississippi, and many school systems were not taking any actions to comply with *Brown*. New Orleans, Louisiana, had bomb threats, boycotts, and KKK demonstrations as the city attempted school desegregation. Several thousand KKK members were on hand to insure failure in the Albany, Georgia, desegregation efforts.[27] Prince Edward County, Virginia, was opening its "private schools" for whites for the fourth year.

The desegregation of schools was also reflecting some of the emotional repercussions of the anxieties involved with desegregation of lunch counters, other major civil rights movements, as well as the concerns with the Cuban crisis. The cautious approach the board was taking probably reflected the feelings and concerns of their constituents, as no one, white or black, wanted violence.

On March 2, 1964, the US Sixth Circuit Court of Appeals dismissed the plaintiffs' appeal of June 7, 1963. The case was remanded to the district court to "effectuate" the decision. On March 18, 1964, an Agreed Order was issued that ". . . the Board of Education of the City of Knoxville shall file a plan as ordered by the Court of Appeals by June 5, 1964, which shall be effective by the time the regular school sessions begin in September, 1964."[28]

At the regular meeting of the board on May 11, 1964, the superintendent recommended the Plan for Complete Desegregation of Public Schools of the City of Knoxville, Tennessee.

The board approved the plan and submitted it to the court on May 20, 1964. The plan was short and straightforward:

1. Effective with the beginning of the school year in September 1964 all twelve grades and curricular offerings of this school system shall be conducted without racial discrimination.

2. Each student will be assigned to the school designated for the district in which he or she legally resides, subject to variations due to overcrowding and other transfers for cause.

3. A plan of school districting based upon the location and capacity (size) of school buildings and the latest enrollment studies will be followed subject to modifications from time to time as required.

4. Requests for transfer of students from the school of their district to another school will be given full consideration and will be granted when made in writing by parents or guardians or those acting in the position of parents, when good cause therefor [*sic*] is shown and when transfer is practicable, consistent with sound school administration.

5. Students may request transfer to or enrollment in any vocational or technical facility sponsored by the Knoxville City Board of Education and will be accepted subject to requirements respecting aptitude, ability, pre-training, physical condition, age, employment opportunities, and other considerations including adequacy of facilities.[29]

The board action was reported in both newspapers. The *Knoxville News-Sentinel* reported: "Full Integration Plan for City Schools OK'd" with a subtitle: "Negro Leaders Want Rule Applied to Teachers, Also."[30] The *Knoxville Journal* reported on another problem: "School Rezoning May Be Avoided." This referred to the enrollment shifts caused by the Urban Renewal project in the Mountain View area. Rather than changing zone lines, the project was only partially complete. Superintendent Johnston would attempt to get parents to voluntarily send their youngsters to Eastport or some other school. Evidence was presented that the population was moving closer to East High School. The same article also carried a subtitle: "Total Desegregation Plan Approved."[31]

Plaintiffs filed Specifications of Objections to the plan on June 11, 1964. Some objections were:

1. That the plan does not meet the requirement of the Fourteenth Amendment to the Constitution of the United States or of the mandate of the United States Court of Appeals for the Sixth Circuit issued on February 20, 1964. . . . Said plan does not provide for the assignment of teachers, principals and other staff and operating personnel and for the general operation of faculty programs on a non-racial basis, nor does it provide for the allotment of funds, construction of schools, and approval of school budgets on a non-racial basis and for the elimination of all considerations of race in any aspect or facet of the school system.

2. The plan does not include as an exhibit a zoning map showing the proposed non-racial school zones to be adopted by the defendants so as to permit a determination by the Court that said proposed zone lines meet the Constitutional requirement for the elimination of all racial considerations in establishment of same.

3. The provisions of the plan relating to transfers and transfer requests are too vague and ambiguous.

4. The plan fails to meet the requirement of the Fourteenth Amendment in that opportunities for transfer or enroll-ment in technical or vocational facilities may be

conditioned upon requirements respecting employment opportunities and other considerations in a community which has a general custom and practice of segregation and discrimination against Negroes in employment opportunities and most aspects of its economic and social life.

5. The plan does not provide for adequate notice to the parents of all Negro and white school children in the City of Knoxville of the respective schools to which their children are assigned and required to attend under the plan.

6. The plan fails to contain a provision reaffirming the retention of jurisdiction of this Court pending complete implementation of desegregation in the City of Knoxville School System.[32]

The board's attorney filed a reply to plaintiffs' objections to the plan submitted to the court on October 29, 1964. Fowler's reply was:

First. The objections are premature. The plan filed by the Board of Education provides for conducting the schools without racial discrimination. Plaintiffs do not aver any specific racially discriminatory action by the board or any justification for anticipating such action.

Second. The objections seek to enlarge the plan by loading it down with details of administration relating to personnel, funds, construction, budgets, zones, notices, etc. Such directions as to details are not properly a part of the plan itself. Moreover, they will unjustifiably interfere with the authority and ability of the Board of Education and its staff to administer the school system, particularly in the absence of any showing that illegal discrimination has occurred or is about to occur.

Third. The filing of these objections without factual justification is unfortunate at this particular time. As plaintiffs well know, the Board of Education and its staff are struggling with serious problems due to the addition of schools in the large area annexed by the city, the ironing out of relations with the Knox County Board of Education, financial needs, the number and location of school population, staffing and other factors. The present superintendent of schools took office only recently on September 1, 1964, and is new to the problems of this city. No justification exists for diverting attention from other demanding needs of the school system to meet the vague objections filed by the plaintiffs.[33]

No court actions appear on the docket for the remainder of the year. The board, with newly appointed Superintendent Dr. Olin L. Adams Jr., staff, and all administrative personnel, were busy complying with the Civil Rights Act of 1964 and following the latest decision of the court as related to the Plan for Complete Desegregation of the Knoxville City Schools.

Not included in the plan to desegregate but by administrative necessity, the board closed three small elementary schools (Happy Home, Lyons View, and Oakland) effective with the beginning of the 1965–66 school year. Students, faculty, and staff were reassigned to remaining schools.

The first political campaign to consolidate the city and county school systems occurred in 1966. Severe budget problems resulting in teacher sanctions, a student march on Knoxville City Hall, and several demonstrations in the communities brought future planning to a literal standstill. Articles in both the *Knoxville Journal* and the *Knoxville News-Sentinel* chronicled the budget problems that precipitated the teacher sanctions. It became apparent that the Knoxville community was divided in many ways over a multitude of issues.

Superintendent (1964–71) Olin L. Adams Jr. Photo courtesy of the Knox County Museum of Education.

Teacher sanctions led to an investigation by the National Education Association. (See appendix D.) The report that followed in March of 1967 was less than complimentary to the Knoxville City Council, the Knoxville Board of Education, the Chamber of Commerce, and both newspapers. It commented on the actions of some Knox County officials in a non-complimentary fashion. The report sums up the situation with the statement:

> Factionalism dominates educational decision making in Knoxville. The [Knoxville] Board of Education is split on nearly every major issue, as is the City Council. The Board minority's dissent from the majority is featured in the local press. The publicly elected county superintendent of schools, an active participant in efforts to consolidate the city schools into the county system, also is a major factor in this controversy.[34]

City council was actively attempting to get rid of the school system. Some members of the board supported these efforts. Desegregating the schools on a greater scale would be a task that teachers and administrators of the system would have to accomplish without the support of these elected bodies.

Although this case stayed on the docket for another ten years, the management and day-to-day operation of the Knoxville city schools was as that of a unitary system. In fact, the system was declared fully desegregated in 1963–64.[35]

Plaintiffs' arguments, from this point forward, would be concerned with whether or not the board was maintaining a unitary system as defined by the most recent court decisions in other jurisdictions. Many adjustments would be made in the next few years. The plaintiffs objected to most of the adjustments for various reasons. The objections would have the effect of speeding up the desegregation process by keeping the decisions of other courts "on the table" in the *Goss* case.

A "unitary school system" would eventually be defined by the courts and the Office of Civil Rights (OCR), but at this time neither the courts nor OCR had a consistent definition.

CHAPTER 4

CIVIL RIGHTS ACT AND COURT SUPERVISION

A S THE *GOSS* CASE PROGRESSED, S. Frank Fowler Sr. was moving toward retirement and his son, Sam F. Fowler Jr., was taking a larger role in the proceedings. The new superintendent of schools, Dr. Olin L. Adams Jr., was adjusting his staff to handle what was becoming a labor intensive part of school administration. A member of the superintendent's staff was assigned as director of research and development with primary responsibilities in the areas of federal compliance and desegregation requirements. This staff member would carry the responsibilities of explaining the desegregation orders of the court to the board and representing the board in the court hearings for the remainder of the litigation.

All school systems across Tennessee were required to file "assurance of compliance" with federal regulations under Title VI of the Civil Rights Act of 1964. Those systems under court orders were treated differently from systems not in litigation. Superintendents in Tennessee were trying to qualify for government-sponsored programs such as vocational education, science education, and staff development that had previously been accepted, but now depended on the paperwork required to qualify. A memorandum from J. Howard Warf, state commissioner of education, mailed on January 8, 1965, illustrates the frustration felt by school administrators as well by the Tennessee Department of Education staff.

TO: All County, City and Special School District
     Superintendents

FROM: J. H. Warf, State Commissioner of Education

SUBJECT: Compliance with Title VI of the Civil Rights
          Act of 1964

Enclosed find copies of form, explanations and instructions for your school system to use in submitting assurance of compliance with Federal regulations under Title VI of the Civil Rights Act of 1964. Compliance with these Federal regulations, by each local school system, is necessary in order for the system to be eligible for continued Federal financial assistance.

These materials were discussed by me with the superintendents in Nashville on January 7, 1965.

As you will see from reading these materials, a school system may comply in one if three ways, viz:

1. By completing and submitting the required number of HEW Form 441, Assurance of Compliance.
2. By filing at least two copies of a plan of desegregation.
3. By filing at least two copies of the latest Federal Court order having to do with the desegregation in your school system.

The method your board of education chooses for compliance should be submitted to this office no later than February 8, 1965. In the event your school system has not filed an assurance of compliance, court order, or plan of desegregation by the above date, it will be assumed that your board of education is not willing to comply with the Civil Rights Act.[1]

It needs to be noted here that existing federal funds were at stake, budgets were being formulated across the state, and members of all the boards took an oath when they took office to uphold the Constitution and obey the laws of the state and federal governments. At best this was a "shotgun choice," and at worst it could mean losing the federal monies expected for vocational and trades programs. It could also mean that a system would lose some, if not all, state funds as well.

Early in 1965, it became evident that this would be a year of intense desegregation activity. On January 19, Superintendent Adams sent a letter to Frank Fowler saying that the board had directed him to request a critique of the Civil Rights Act of 1964 as it affected the current status of the desegregation plan. On that same day, Fowler filed with the court a Motion for Pre-trial Conference for the scheduled February 1965 hearing. The motion illustrated the confusion that was developing with school administration, court orders, and requirements of the Civil Rights Act of 1964, as interpreted by HEW. In part, the motion stated:

> Comes the defendant Board of Education of the City of Knoxville, Tennessee, and moves the court for a pre-trial conference of this case, and to that end that the parties be directed to appear before the court for a conference to consider:
>
> 1. The simplification of the issues;
> 2. The possibility of obtaining stipulations and admissions of fact and of documents which will avoid unnecessary proof;
> 3. Such other matters as may aid in the disposition of the issues presented.
>
> Defendants show that trial is now set for February 26, 1965, upon the Specification of Objections of the plaintiffs to the defendant's plan of desegregation and that the objections are undoubtedly much broader than any illegal discriminations

that plaintiffs can or will seek to develop at the hearing; that the statutory law possibly applicable to this case has been enhanced by the enactment of the Civil Rights Act of 1964, and the applicability and significance of this statute and Government action pursuant thereto, both State and Federal, must be determined as matter of law; . . .[2]

Fowler responded to Adams's letter of January 19 in a letter dated January 26, 1965, with the following observations:

The right to terminate or deny Federal funds is granted to each Federal department or agency through which such distributions are made. . . . The following indicate pertinent provisions of the Act—that is, the really salient provisions;

HEW is authorized by regulations to effectuate Section 601 of Title 6, being 42 USCA, Section 2000d, reading as follows;

"No person in the United States shall, on the ground of race, color, or national origin, be excluded from participation in, be denied the benefits of, or be subjected to discrimination under any program or activity receiving Federal financial assistance."

The regulations of HEW applicable to our problem seek to obtain compliance with the above quoted section by control of Federal moneys.

It is noted, however, that compliance can be enforced "by any other means authorized by law," which is a flexible provision inviting the ingenuity of HEW and other Federal agencies to achieve compliance.[3]

With budget development in process for the 1965–66 school year, the board had a "full plate." Several applications for special federal projects were waiting for funding decisions. The Tennessee Department of Education was being very vague about resources from the state level. Annexation of eighteen schools was a reality for September 1965 and some community groups were still urging the merger of the city and county school systems. The motion for a pre-trial conference was a sincere attempt to settle some of the issues, answer some questions, and to decide what issues, if any, would go to trial.

The pre-trial conference was held on February 5, 1965, resulting in modifications to both the plan presented by the board and the list of objections filed by the plaintiffs. On the day of the conference, Fowler sent a letter to the superintendent outlining the changes and amendments to the plan which had been submitted to the court on May 20, 1964.[4] The first item of the original plan was practically rewritten, some minor adjustments were made to paragraphs two through five, and a sixth paragraph was added. The Agreed Order was filed on February 12, 1965, with additional tasks added by the court. The board was directed to "utilize its best efforts to lay-out and portray, by suitable mapping, school district lines which shall be drawn in conformity with Paragraph 1 of the Plan of Desegregation as amended and to file the same by April 1, 1965."[5]

The superintendent's staff immediately began work on the changes required by the Agreed Order and incorporated the amendments into the original plan. The amended plan was approved by the board on February 8, 1965, and presented to the court on February 16, 1965. The new plan was as follows:

1. Effective with the beginning of the school year in September, 1964, all racially discriminatory practices in all grades, programs and facilities of the Knoxville Public School System shall be eliminated and abolished. Without limiting the generality and effectiveness of the foregoing, all teachers, principals and other school personnel shall be employed by defendants and assigned or re-assigned to schools on the basis of educational need and other academic considerations, and without regard to race or color of the person to be assigned, and without regard to

the race or color of the children attending the particular school or class within a school to which the person is to be assigned. No transfer or re-transfer of a teacher, principal or other school personnel may be granted or required for considerations based upon race and color and no assignment or reassignment of such teacher, principal or other school personnel may be made for considerations based upon race or color.

2. Each student will be assigned to the school designated for the district in which he or she legally resides, subject to variations due to overcrowding and other transfers for cause.

3. A plan of school districting based upon the location and capacity (size) of school buildings and the latest enrollment studies will be followed subject to modifications from time to time as required.

4. Requests for transfer of students from the school of their district to another school will be given full consideration and will be granted when made in writing by parents or guardians or those acting in the position of parents, when good cause therefor [*sic*] is shown and when transfer is practicable, consistent with sound school administration.

5. Students may request transfer to or enrollment in any vocational or technical facility sponsored by the Knoxville City Board of Education and will be accepted subject to requirements respecting aptitude, ability, pre-training, physical condition, age, and other considerations including adequacy of facilities.

6. The Board of Education recognizes the continuation of jurisdiction of the United States District Court for the Eastern District of Tennessee, Northern Division, at Knoxville of the Board and the matters involved in this plan, until termination of said jurisdiction by express direction of said court.[6]

Plaintiffs' Specifications of Objections to the amended plan for complete desegregation was filed with the court on February 23, 1965. These objections were related to the zoning maps directed in the Agreed Order which would make the plan premature and give the court no means of determining whether the plan met the constitutional test. The plaintiffs asked:

> That said paragraphs 2, 3, 4 of the defendants' amended plan for complete desegregation be disapproved and that further action on the entire plan be held in abeyance until the incoming of defendants' zoning map and revised transfer plan not later than April 1965.[7]

Developing the attendance zone maps was a labor intensive and difficult process. No computerized attendance figures, current official maps, or up-to-date census figures were available. Maps used in the annexation process contained census zones and voting districts that did not match school attendance zones. New road construction and Urban Renewal projects complicated the process even more. The entire process was manual!

The board filed an application on April 2, 1965, for additional time to complete the zone maps. The map was completed and submitted to the court on April 27, 1965. This delivery was considered a partial compliance with the Agreed Order because only one copy was made available. Additional copies were made available on May 7, 1965.

Plaintiffs objected to the zones, the process for developing them, and results they produced. There were still majority black schools and majority white schools, reflecting the racial makeup of the communities. The plaintiffs were not the only ones unhappy with the zones adopted by the board.

A letter to the editor of the *Knoxville News-Sentinel* described the plan as: "School zoning plan for Knoxville a miscarriage of justice . . . Obviously, neighborhoods tend to become economic ghettos, if not racial ones; therefore neighborhood zoning tends to defeat the ideals of integration and total equality of educational opportunity."[8]

To add to the mix of troublesome processes, Superintendent Adams received a letter from the supervisor of the Trade and Industrial Education programs in Tennessee saying that applications for two programs were being put on hold "until Knoxville was adjudged to be in full compliance with the law." Knoxville was left off the approved list. No reason was given as to why, or what was needed to be in "full compliance." Newspaper headlines read: "Knoxville Blackballed by HEW"[9]

On May 21, 1965, Carl Cowan, plaintiffs' attorney, asked for additional time to file objections to the attendance areas and procedural policies. Further Specifications of Objections to the amended plan for complete desegregation were filed with the court on June 18, 1965. These objections were added to the ones made earlier and were more inclusive. When the board submitted the zone plans and other papers to comply with the order of February 12, 1965, the provision for a student to stay in the school to which he/she was attending until the student completed the grades housed in that school was included.

Cowan took exception to this provision and made it his first objection in the further Specifications of Objections. The remainder of the objections referred to the inadequacy and vagueness of the entire plan. He asked the court to:

1. Set an early date to open all the plaintiffs' objections to the Amended Plan for Complete Desegregation of the Knoxville City Schools.
2. Disapprove paragraphs 2, 3, and 4 of the plan.
3. Disapprove the zone maps and all papers filed with them.
4. Modify the plan to (a) . . . require all students in the Knoxville School System to enroll in and attend the schools in which assigned under a unitary nonracial zoning system beginning with the school year 1965–66; (b) To require defendants to assure timely, adequate and full notice to parents and students of their rights under the general plan of complete desegregation . . . (c) To require

that the defendants permit students to transfer to schools outside their assigned attendance zones only in exceptional cases for objective reasons to be specifically set forth ... (d) To require all pupils attending school outside their assigned attendance zone to obtain approval of the superintendent of schools ...

5. That, after action of the court upon all of the foregoing, the complete plan of desegregation for the Knoxville School System, as heretofore and hereafter approved by the Court, be embodied in a single document which shall set forth in a cogent manner all provisions of said plan.[10]

Item One of the plan having to do with the hiring, placement, transfer, and re-transfer would become problematic when it became necessary to manage the race ratio of faculty in every school.

Judge Taylor set a hearing for August 3, 1965. A pre-trial conference was held on July 28, 1965. Arguments were heated and very adversarial during the conference. The *Knoxville Journal* reported: "Desegregation Suit Hearing Vexes Judge." Avon Williams, plaintiffs' attorney, was quoted: "The court has delayed in the enjoyment of our rights for six years." Judge Taylor came back with: "The court has not delayed you in anything. Don't make a statement like that here."[11] Williams pushed for the court to require the board to make annual reports of desegregation progress to the court. Judge Taylor replied: "There has to be an end to this lawsuit and I don't expect to continue to have these meetings."[12]

After Williams told the court it "still is dealing with a substantially segregated school system here," Fowler responded: "This business of trying to run a school system without administrative experience seems to me to be utterly silly." Later he said the plaintiffs were "trying to lay down a cast-iron set of statements for this board to go by. They are trying to write a charter here to govern pupils in city schools. All of this talk assumes that this board is going to be biased and dedicated to segregation, and that is utterly false."[13]

The Agreed Order was transmitted to the superintendent the next day. The order struck paragraph three from the plan submitted by the board and substituted the following:

> Upon written application, students may be permitted to transfer to schools outside their assigned attendance zones only in exceptional cases for objective administrative reasons and no transfer shall be granted, denied or required because of race or color.

The plan was further amended by striking paragraph four and substituting the following:

> All applications of students for transfers to schools outside their assigned attendance zones shall be considered and approved by the Superintendent of schools at his discretion pursuant to recommendations of the Director of the Department of Child Personnel after due investigation and consideration of the Department of Child Personnel.[14]

The Agreed Order further directed the board to "publicize the desegregation plan as amended."

Lawyers on neither side could agree on the grade-completion clause of the plan. The *Knoxville News-Sentinel* carried an article that said this case had been to the US Sixth Circuit Court of Appeals twice and the Supreme Court once with only portions affirmed and always sent back to the District Court in Knoxville for further proceedings. The article also quoted Williams as asking the court to require the board "be directed to set forth a rigid set of rules which provide that a student 'must attend a school in his zone . . . .'"[15]

The grade-completion clause remained one unresolved issue to go to trial on August 3, 1965. Plaintiffs' counsel stated that it would be impossible to prepare for a hearing at such an early date. The standing court date was deferred until such time as the court could find an open date. The board was given full authority to follow the plan of desegregation as amended by the Agreed Order.[16] Judge Taylor signed the Agreed Order on July 30, 1965. Before signing the order, however, he struck out a paragraph requiring the board to file annual reports.

The board submitted the revised plan, which presented all the elements of the plan in one document, on August 6, 1965. (See appendix C.) The superintendent issued a press release describing the amended transfer policy. Newspapers reported the plan as: "Desegregation Plan Okehed By US Judge"[17] and "School Mixing Agreement OK'd."[18] Both accounts indicated that all issues had been resolved except the issue of "students who are attending school outside their assigned zone and remaining in that school until completing the grades contained therein."

Although this issue remained, the "freedom of choice" transfer was no longer in existence and the list of reasons for requesting transfers had been eliminated. Transfers would hereafter be granted: ". . . in exceptional cases for objective administrative reasons and no transfer shall be granted, denied or required because of race or color."[19]

The *Knoxville News-Sentinel* carried an article on August 12, 1965, titled: "School Switch Deadline Tuesday." The article stated that anyone who wanted to attend a school out of the assigned zone must make application for transfer under the new board policy. In the event that the application was denied by the superintendent, a hearing of all appeals would be scheduled on August 23, 1965.[20] This announcement was followed with another article: "400 Pupil Transfers Requested."[21] Superintendent Adams was quoted as saying that transfers would not be granted unless there is "a real hardship or safety factor involved." He was concerned that to do otherwise would "leave some question about whether or not we are complying with the intent of the court."[22]

Administering the transfer and zoning issues remained a difficult problem. On August 23, 1965, the board held an executive session for the purpose of discussing the transfer provisions of the court-approved plan. The discussion centered on the situation many families, both black and white, were experiencing. If an older child had been given a transfer to a school outside the assigned zone and was still in that school under the grade-completion rule and a younger sibling becomes of school age, could the younger child get a transfer to the school the older child is attending? The situation of one child going to one school and the other child going to a different school was causing problems with families all over the city. The discussion led to the adoption of what would be labeled the "brother-sister" transfer. This transfer allowed the younger child to follow the older sibling.[23]

Plaintiffs' attorneys took exception to the brother-sister policy. Carl Cowan wrote a letter to Frank Fowler on October 2, 1965, stating:

> The attorneys for the plaintiffs have expected to get a copy of said amendment; and that an application would be made by the Board of Education to the Court for approval of said amendment to its declaration of policy made on April 19, 1965, notwithstanding this change has been in operation without Court approval since the beginning of the 1965–1966 school year.
>
> In our opinion, such action is contrary and inconsistent with the letter and spirit of Section 2 of the procedural policies of said declaration, and violated the equal protection and due process clauses of the Fourteenth Amendment to the Constitution of the United States . . . [24]

Fowler responded two days later:

> . . . When this school year opened the Board of Education, as I recall, was besieged by complaints and entreaties from various parents particularly in newly annexed areas, to obtain relief on transportation problems as well as perhaps other benefits, completely unrelated to racial considerations—these

applications were being made by parents for the purpose of getting their young children, newly starting, into the same schools where older children were going. The Board consulted me on the matter and since no racial involvement appeared, I told them in my opinion it was within their power to grant the applications.[25]

Superintendent Adams received a copy of Fowler's letter with a copy of Cowan's letter enclosed, and on October 4, 1965, returned a copy of the board's August 23 action. On November 2, 1965, Fowler forwarded a copy of the board action to Cowan with the notation: "I shall appreciate your advice on this action of the Board. It was not intended to have any relation whatever to the issues of our case, as I understand the matter."[26]

Most of the plaintiffs' concerns were centered on the transfer policies and practices, but the board had other concerns. Budget problems were severe. Teachers invoked sanctions. (See appendix D.) There was a second referendum to consolidate the school system with Knox County school system. Regulations produced by the 1964 Civil Rights Act were coming from HEW on a weekly basis.

The school year of 1965–66 saw the beginning of faculty mixing. The guidelines from HEW, as well as recent court decisions, indicated that the faculty in each school must reflect, as close as possible, the general population. Prior to this date there had been interracial assignments of faculty, mostly afforded by the opportunity of vacancies or transfers of convenience, but there had been no attempt to desegregate all faculties on a fixed ratio.

The desegregation plans submitted to and approved by the court dealt mostly with students—their access to an interracial environment and access to programs—and only generally with all other phases of school operation. The Sixth Circuit Court of Appeals upheld Judge Taylor's approval of the plan submitted by the board. However, it was remanded to the district court for judgment as to whether or not the board was complying with the *Swann v. Charlotte-Mecklenburg* decision. The board would now have to consider the elements of that decision in comparison to Knoxville's desegregation progress. The big concern was with the busing that had been ordered in the *Swann* decision.

Faculty desegregation had a slow start. Attempting to adhere to the mandates of the *Swann* decision was difficult. The demographics and legal history of the two systems were entirely different. To ensure that all faculties would be structured to reflect the racial composition of the community meant that 85 percent of black faculty but only 15 percent of white faculty would be subject to transfer. The detrimental effects on the traditional black faculties were readily apparent and there was the board policy of not hiring, assigning, or transferring based on race that had to be considered.

The administrative staff decided to go about the mixing of faculties by first filling vacancies with newly hired teachers of the appropriate race to meet the percentage required in that school. This worked reasonably well in the elementary schools and in some junior high and high schools, but availability of black teachers soon became a problem. An exchange method was adopted. A teacher of one race was selected to be exchanged for a teacher of the other race on a school-by-school, grade-by-grade basis. It seemed to be a simple process, but considering grade level, licensure requirements, and physical restrictions of teachers really complicated the process.

Certain teachers had to be excluded (such as coaches, librarians, shop teachers, band directors, and music teachers) because of licensure and continuing program requirements. After a long and tedious summer, very few schools had a faculty mix that met the goal of representing the race mixture of the community. No principals were reassigned or employed based on race. Teachers were still being hired and assigned on the basis of need and licensure requirements.

The process continued every year until the faculty mix in all schools was in an acceptable range by final "lottery" in 1971. To the credit of both the teachers that were assigned to the schools and those teachers in the receiving schools, the faculty desegregation effort was relatively successful.

The director of personnel and development directed the faculty assignments. He teamed with Dr. Roy Wallace, director of instruction; Tom Underwood, supervisor of elementary education; Dr. Earl Henry, supervisor of secondary education; Harry Gillespie, director of federal projects; and principals to select the teachers to be transferred. The time and effort were taken to ensure the proper professional and personality fit in as many transfer situations as possible. Most of the transfers went well, some transfers were difficult, and a few were initially absolute disasters.

The role principals played in preparing for the race balancing of faculty was a major factor to the success of the effort. Not all were successful in fully preparing their faculty. A few didn't try, but the vast majority of principals, teachers, staff, and other personnel were prepared and cooperative.

Dr. Paul Kelley, principal of West High School, was a prime example of the way most principals prepared their faculties. He simply stated that whoever was sent to West High School would be professionally qualified and assigned in the same fashion that the existing faculty had been assigned. They would be treated accordingly and they were.

Ruth Benn was one of the black teachers sent to West. She had been a guidance counselor at Vine Junior for several years. Knowing that most of the students at West were white, she approached Kelley with, "How do you want me to work with the students here?" He replied, "The same way you have worked with students at Vine, and I will back you." Benn not only worked well with the West High students, she became known as the social planner for the faculty.

On the other end of the spectrum, a black elementary teacher, Dessa Blair, was sent to a white school where the principal was not too keen on the whole process. She was first placed in the hall, behind some file cabinets, and then assigned to a portable classroom not attached to the main building. Although there was always a strained relationship with the principal, he did recognize her excellent teaching. Within a year they recognized Martin Luther King week with posters, student art work, and school-wide activities. In a short time, parents were requesting that their children be assigned to her class.

On December 13, 1965, Mr. Fowler notified the superintendent that a hearing had been set for February 8, 1966, with the main considerations being those students who attend a school outside their zone because they had been going to that school, and ". . . there will be reviewed the practice of letting little brother or sister go there."

Legal maneuvering began early in 1966. Plaintiffs filed interrogatories on January 17, 1966, and followed on January 19, 1966, with amendments to the Specifications of Objections to the amended plan for complete desegregation filed by the board. Fowler sent a letter to Cowan on January 25, 1966, that indicated that the trial date for the *Goss* case had been rescheduled from February 8, 1966, to March 22, 1966. He also mentioned that the superintendent's staff was having trouble responding to the interrogatories: "As soon as the staff of the school board gets through with the big push on the budget, they will take up the interrogatories which you have put to the school superintendent."

Superintendent Adams followed with a letter dated March 2 to Fowler:

> We are presently in process of compiling information as requested in the Plaintiff Interrogatory. Certainly, we shall make every effort to comply with requested information pertinent to this case. However, strict adherence to these requests will require very meticulous examination of records and individual listing of some six to seven thousand pupils attending school outside their prescribed school zones.
>
> In view of these considerations, we would request permission to include this information in chart form. If this request is considered we shall be glad to make available to the court and/or plaintiff lawyers any available information relative to points under consideration.[27]

Fowler then followed with a motion filed with the court on March 5, 1966, "to limit scope of interrogatories." Defendants replied by filing more interrogatories on March 15, 1966. These interrogatories were not just a series of questions; they were, in fact, subpoenas for massive amounts of data. For example, the first subpoena had eighteen questions; each question had up to eight parts; most had to be answered by race; and if it involved transfers, the reason for the transfer had to be included.

On September 11, 1966, a petition was filed against Superintendent Adams and members of the board by the parents of Billy Ray Hancock challenging his assignment to Vine Junior High School on the basis that Park Junior High School was closer to his home. The case was originally filed in Knox County Chancery Court but was removed to federal court on September 29, 1966. The complaint did not question desegregation, since Billy Ray had been attending Park City-Lowry Elementary (a desegregated student body). It was only a distance problem. A temporary injunction was issued requiring enrollment at Park Junior until a hearing was scheduled at a later date.[28] The case was dismissed on May 23, 1967.

The court docket sheet indicates no other court action or filings until March 1, 1967, when the plaintiffs filed more interrogatories. More than a dozen interrogatories would be issued before the case ended. Evidence was presented in a hearing that interrogatories cost the school system approximately $50,000 to produce in the mid-1960s.

On March 7, 1967, the board voted to establish free summer schools at Austin, Fulton, Rule, West, and Young High Schools; Beaumont, Ft. Sanders, Green, Lonsdale, Maynard, and McCallie Elementary Schools; and the Knoxville Evening High School. These sessions were funded by federal funds provided by the Elementary and Secondary Education Act (ESEA) of 1965. Previous summer sessions had been fee based.

A pre-trial conference was held in district court on March 10, 1967, resulting in a pre-trial order stating the issues:

1. Whether or not the provision in amendment dated April 19, 1965 to the Knoxville school desegregation plan for

continued enrollment of students in their present schools until completion of grade requirements for said schools violates the Fourteenth Amendment to the United States Constitution and is inadequate and improper as a part of the Knoxville School Desegregation Plan in that it perpetuates racial segregation and delays integration of the school system.

2. Whether or not the provision in amendment dated August 23, 1965 to the Knoxville School Desegregation Plan permitting children of the same family to transfer to and attend schools out of their zone of residence where a brother or sister might otherwise be required to attend different schools violates the Fourteenth Amendment to the United States Constitution and is inadequate and improper as a part of the Knoxville School Desegregation Plan in that it perpetuates racial segregation and delays integration of the school system.

3. In the operation of the plan has the School Board effectively complied with the Fourteenth Amendment as far as desegregation of the school is concerned in relation to the matters referred to in Issues 1 and 2.[29]

The plaintiffs filed exceptions to the pre-trial order on March 27, 1967. Judge Taylor denied the plaintiffs' exceptions and motion to further amend the pre-trial order on May 3. Findings of Fact, motions for further relief, defendants' briefs, depositions, and responses to interrogatories took up all of April and the first part of May 1967.

The trial began on May 11, but was adjourned until May 15. Both days consisted of the board's attorney presenting evidence that the schools were being administered according to the desegregation plan and the building of new facilities was not an effort to continue segregation.

This was the first trial in which Sam F. Fowler Jr. had the primary role of presenting the evidence and witnesses. He was well prepared and had been involved in the case for several years. His arguments consisted of explaining the board's response to previous court orders and the voluntary actions that had been taken by the board to further progress toward desegregation of the school system.

However, he had a personal vocabulary and diction flaw that caused a stir. Sam Fowler grew up in an affluent family who employed domestic help. It was the custom, as a respectful gesture, to refer to a Negro as "negra" rather than "nigger" or black. In one of the early arguments he used the word "negra." Avon Williams came out of his chair like a rocket: "If Your Honor please, if I were to call Mr. Fowler by an insulting name and kept doing it, I am sure the Court would call me down. I am in a court of law and expect people of my ethnic group especially, that is very crucial, we are here on a hearing because of the problem of people refusing to recognize the rights and feelings of other people. I respectfully expect and request that Mr. Fowler be admonished to correctly pronounce the word 'Negro.'"

Mr. Fowler responded: "I am afraid I am going to have to use 'colored.' I will do my best."

Judge Taylor instructed Mr. Fowler, "Do your best to say 'Negro.'"

Mr. Fowler responded, "I apologize to him profusely. I am afraid that I am a victim of my own surroundings."

During a short recess later in the day, Fowler asked Williams, "Is it OK if I say 'black'?" Williams said, "Yes." Fowler never used the word "negra" in court for the duration of the case.

The incident did make an impression on Fowler. During a speech to the Knoxville Bar Association in 2011, he admonished young attorneys, "Be careful with your language in sensitive cases." He illustrated his remark with the story of the incident with Avon Williams.

The plaintiffs presented argument supporting the motion that defendants be restrained from proceeding with the construction of two new high schools. The court allowed plaintiffs to file the motion in writing at which time the court would act on the motion. The case was taken under advisement.

On June 7, 1967, Judge Taylor issued an order that the various objections to the school plan be denied. He ordered that the motion for an injunction enjoining the building of proposed schools in the Bearden and Fountain City areas be denied. In a memorandum opinion, Judge Taylor ruled that "the school authorities are moving skillfully and with expedition toward the full integration of the Knoxville School System, that there is no further need for the schools to operate under Court supervision."[30] He further ordered the case stricken from the docket.

The plaintiffs appealed the decision on June 19, 1967, and on September 8, 1967, the case file was mailed to the US Court of Appeals Sixth Circuit, Cincinnati, Ohio. No further activity appeared on the court docket until early 1969.

The school system continued to operate under the June 7, 1967, decision of the district court. At the February 1968 regular board meeting, the superintendent brought to the attention of the board that Austin High School had lost enrollment, even though new vocational facilities had been completed. He recommended that Austin High School be discontinued and combined with East High School. East High School would house the academic classes, and the vocational classes would be taught in the Austin High facility.

The superintendent was concerned with the mix of school organization that had resulted over the years because of overcrowding and the annexation of schools with different organization patterns. He recommended that effective with the 1968–69 school year the ninth grade be dropped from East, Fulton, and West High Schools. Students in these grades would be assigned to the appropriate junior high schools.[31]

On March 11, 1968, the board designated Austin High School vocational division (the new addition on the Bertrand Street side of the school) as East High School Vocational Center and the remainder of the facility as Knoxville Adult Center and Knoxville Evening High School. Austin High School no longer existed.

This decision was one that probably had to be made, but it would be one of the casualties of the desegregation of the school system.

At the next regular board meeting on April 15, Rev. R. E. Stephens appeared before the board to object to dropping the name of Austin. In a unanimous decision, the board renamed the vocational center and East High School as Austin-East High School.[32]

The 1968 Knoxville Board of Education. The last five-member board (from left to right, standing): Charles R. Burchett and Lewis S. Howard; (seated): John S. Humphreys, W. Howard Temple, and Lynn W. Craig. Photo courtesy of Fred Bedelle Jr.

The fall session of 1968 experienced the first freshman class of Austin-East High School. As an integration effort it was a failure. Most of the white students had moved to other school zones; the most pronounced example of "white flight" that Knoxville experienced. However, "white flight" cannot be given all the blame for the influx of blacks into the Austin-East zone. Urban Renewal projects, funded by various government agencies, had moved the entire black community eastward, closer to the old East High School.

It soon became very evident that the board had little ability to stabilize the population and/or race balance in the peripheral areas of the city. School capacity was being strained in the outer school zones and lack of enrollment in the old city school buildings was causing problems. The city did not have a transportation system and there was a real possibility that the entire school system would be "out of business" in the near future because of continuing consolidation efforts.

CHAPTER 5

1969 TO 1971—THE CLIMAX

A MANDATE AND OPINION OF THE Sixth Circuit Court of Appeals affirming the June 7, 1967, judgment of the district court (that the Knoxville School System was in compliance with the *Swann* decision except that the district court is directed to keep the case on the docket), was filed on March 12, 1969. The plaintiffs had ninety days in which to file a Petition for Certiorari in the US Supreme Court.

Sam Fowler sent a letter on September 2, 1969, to the superintendent's office stating:

> The petitioners in this case were granted until June 11, 1969 to file a petition for certiorari in the Supreme Court. Since they did not take advantage of the extension, the Court of Appeals' opinion is in full force and effect . . . So long as the Knoxville School District continues to make the progress in desegregation that it has made in the past, I believe this case will lie dormant.[1]

Wrong! On September 17, 1969, plaintiffs filed a Motion for Immediate Relief. The plaintiffs' attorney, Avon Williams, asked for relief on grounds of:

1. On information and belief, plaintiffs aver that said desegregation plan adopted by the defendants and approved by

the court in this case has not resulted in a unitary school system in Knoxville, Tennessee . . .

2. . . . the defendants have continued and are continuing to operate, maintain and perpetuate said racially segregated school system in the City of Knoxville, Tennessee, by means of gerrymandered geographic zone lines and by other means, including the planning, designing, locating and construction of new schools and additions or extensions of existing schools in such manner as to conform to racial residential patterns and to encourage and support the growth of racial segregation in such residential patterns.

3. . . . Federal Courts should order complete and immediate relief which must be implemented at once pending litigation of objections and amendments to plans of desegregation, including review by the Court of Appeals.

4. This litigation has been pending for ten years and prior litigation by Negro plaintiffs was pending before this suit was filed and was dismissed on technical grounds, but plaintiffs and the class have yet to enjoy the benefits of scholastic instruction in a unitary system.

5. Although there is no plan of desegregation drawn by the Department of Health, Education and Welfare presently before this Court, a plan is capable of being devised within a very short period . . .

6. . . . to require the immediate effectuation of a unitary school system in the city of Knoxville, Tennessee, which requires a substantial change in the present racial attendance patterns and elimination of the racial identifiability of the public schools of said city. WHEREFORE plaintiffs respectfully pray that this Court: (a) Reduce defendants' time to respond to this Motion to three (3) days; (b) . . . request the Department of Health, Education and Welfare to craft a plan to achieve immediately a unitary school system. . . . (c) Issue a temporary restraining

order enjoining the defendants immediately from proceeding further with any and all new school construction. ... (d) Proceed promptly to consider and approve a constitutional final plan for the operation of the public schools of the City of Knoxville.... (e) Allow plaintiffs their costs....[2]

The plaintiffs' attorneys would from this point to the end of the case take the position that the system is not unitary as long as there are all-white schools or all-black schools in the system. There would be an aggressive attempt to require busing in order to mix the racial composition in every school.

Fowler prepared a response to the Motion for Immediate Relief and sent it to the superintendent for review, but never filed it with the court.

The headline of the *Knoxville Journal* on October 30, 1969, read: "All Schools Told To Integrate At Once." The first line of the article stated: "The Supreme Court, ordering the immediate desegregation of Mississippi public schools, declared Wednesday night a segregated school system no longer is permissible anywhere in the nation." The Knoxville School System had been declared unitary in 1964, but the case was still on the docket.

Originally Knoxville High School, this building was occupied by the Knoxville Board of Education from 1951 to 1987. It was eventually renamed Historic Knoxville High. Photo courtesy of Fred Bedelle Jr.

The Knoxville Board of Education, as well as other boards throughout the South, was receiving criticism from both sides of the issue. Some very vocal individuals were blaming the Negro for "being used." The editorial page of the *Knoxville News–Sentinel,* Forum Section, contained two letters to the editor. One was titled "Negro Says Many of His Race Need to Help Correct Ills" and stated, ". . . We should not cry long and loud about discrimination when we ourselves continue to develop the attitude of 'if I can't, you will not.' How can we ever have confidence in one another until we merit it?"[3]

The other letter to the editor was titled "Brothers' Keepers Order Negroes Around" and said, "Our Federal and state policy in trying to resolve our racial problem is nothing short of a national disgrace. Every trick in the book is tried in an attempt to defile the highest court in the land, the United States Supreme Court. There will not be any real progress made in resolving this problem until the white man is willing to give to the Negro his chance, his freedom, before the law and before God."[4]

On November 17, 1969, the plaintiffs filed a Motion for Immediate Relief and more interrogatories. A Show Cause Order was issued the same day for December 12, 1969. On November 19, 1969, plaintiffs filed an amendment to the Motion for Immediate Relief plus supplemental interrogatories. The superintendent's staff would work almost two months to prepare answers to these interrogatories.

In addition to the desegregation problems, 1969 presented the board with other concerns. The elections for city officials, including the board, had changed. Rather than running at large, city council and school board candidates were nominated by district, with the top two nominees running at large. The new process, because of housing patterns and voting district zones, assured at least one black member would be elected to each body. Sarah Moore Greene was elected as the first black member of the Knoxville Board of Education. Theotis Robinson Jr. was elected to the Knoxville City Council. Greene had been very active in NAACP activities, having served as local president. Robinson was a plaintiff in the *Goss* case. The board not only had its first black member, it now was a nine-member board as opposed to the former five-member body. The rest of the members of the new board were: Howard Temple, Charles

Burchett, Lynn W. Craig, William "Bill" Carty, Kenneth "Red" Bailes, John Humphreys, Lewis Howard, and Luther Woods.

Court decisions in other cases throughout the South also began to influence the progress on the *Goss* case. The *Swann v. Charlotte-Mechlenberg* decision, which required busing to integrate the system; the *Alexander v. Holmes County Board of Education,* which ordered pairing and closing of schools; and the *Norcross v. Board of Education, Memphis City Schools,* which ordered the use of recommendations of HEW experts ordered by the court were just a few cases that impacted the desegregation efforts. A national definition of a "unitary" system was still evolving in the courts.

The decade of 1970 would see the end of the *Goss* litigation. This period would also be the "beginning of the end" of the Knoxville City School System. Although the two events are not related in the sense of "cause and effect," the attitudes, politics, and financial situations of the city and county government did play a role in some of the board's actions. These events will be noted in the actions of the board only where context is important.

The new Knoxville Board of Education met with Frank Fowler and Sam Fowler on January 19, 1970, to discuss the desegregation progress—lack thereof, related problems, and future directions and plans.

The first nine-member board of education in Knoxville. (From left to right, standing): Kenneth "Red" Bailes, Charles Burchett, John Humphreys, and Bayard Erskine (replaced Lynn Craig); (seated): William "Bill" Carty, Sarah Moore Greene, Luther Woods, Howard Temple, and Lewis Howard. Photo courtesy of Fred Bedelle Jr.

On January 30, 1970, attorneys for the board filed a Motion to Dismiss on the grounds that the issues had been settled and the system had been declared unitary. There was also pending in the court, at this point in time, a Motion for Immediate Relief filed by the plaintiffs.

The board filed answers to the November 1969 interrogatories on February 2, 1970. Plaintiffs filed more interrogatories on February 12, 1970.

The plaintiffs filed opposition to the Motion to Dismiss on February 17. They opposed the Motion to Dismiss on twelve issues:

1. The *Goss* case has been in continuous litigation since December 11, 1959.
2. The school board is continuing to operate a dual school system in contravention to the Constitution.
3. Data indicates that the system has only an "average percentage desegregation of 3.8%."
4. This percentage demonstrates that the Knoxville School system is still segregated.
5. Faculties remain segregated to a substantial degree.
6. The Federal Courts should order complete and immediate relief which must be implemented at once.
7. The system is operating a segregated system by means of gerrymandering zone lines and building facilities in such a way as to perpetuate segregation.
8. Although the District Court approved the integration plan and struck the case from the docket, the Appeals Court did not affirm the District Court's action in striking the case from the docket.
9. If the Motion for Immediate Relief contains anything upon which the plaintiffs could conceivably be entitled to relief, then the defendant's motion should be denied.
10. . . . school children, as to their constitutional rights to attend a racially integrated public school system, must now be afforded immediate relief commensurate with the fundamental importance of their rights involved and with applicable principles of equity.

11. It is no longer sufficient that a plan move toward full integration. And,
12. The defendants should be allowed no further time towards full integration.[5]

Sam Fowler wrote a letter to Superintendent Adams on February 24, responding to instructions given at the January meeting. The letter reflected a change in attitude of the board members and a more proactive defensive position of the attorneys resulting from Sam Fowler having a more prominent role. In part, the letter read:

> At the meeting of the Board which my father and I attended the evening of January 19, 1970, we stated that we would write you a letter summarizing the areas which we thought the Board should carefully study. These problem areas, if not carefully handled, could trigger adverse consequences on the part of the Federal District Court or HEW. In other words, if the school board does not take action itself the court or HEW may order the Board to take actions which will have a detrimental effect on the whole school system. Our experience in the past has been that if the school board itself takes action the Court very likely will approve the action. This is as it should be. The Board owes a duty to the Court in addition to that to the public to administer the system. In the states south of us where the school boards have refused to take any action on their own, the courts have introduced integration plans which have been unreasonable and unworkable. It is therefore our suggestion that the Board give serious consideration to the following areas:
>
> 1. Rule, Beardsley . . .
> 2. Lonsdale, Sam Hill . . .
> 3. Fair Garden, Park Lowry and Park Junior . . .
> 4. Beaumont, Cansler, Maynard and Moses . . .
> 5. Every formerly Negro school in the system should have a mixed student body as soon as possible.
> 6. All school staff should be bi-racial at the earliest possible time.

7. All new school construction should take into consideration this segregation problem.
8. Transfer rules . . .[6]

The concern with Beardsley had to do with the fact that it was the
only school in the system that ended with the tenth grade. In Fowler's
opinion, this organization contributed to some students dropping out at
the tenth grade. Since there were no white students attending Beardsley
at the time, he anticipated it being a serious situation.

The Lonsdale and Sam Hill problem was really a "no brainer." Under
the segregation laws, these two schools were built two blocks apart, one
for blacks and one for whites. Fowler suggested pairing the schools, one
containing grades one through three and the other grades four through
six. At this point, the court had not ordered any pairing, but as Fowler
stated: ". . . in light of the recent Supreme Court decision in *Alexander v.
Holmes County Board of Education*, our time has run out."[7]

Fair Garden, Park Lowry, Park Junior, Beaumont, Cansler,
Maynard, and Moses were well desegregated, but the concern was
"white flight." The pairing of Austin High School and East High
School to form Austin-East High School had been an integration
disaster. Two years after Austin-East was formed, it was over 50 percent
black, and in another two years, 99 percent black. White families had
either moved out of the community or they had enrolled their children
in the closest county school. Fowler was adamant that something
should be done to prevent the same thing happening again: "These
schools should be mixed more, but care should be taken not to drive
whites from the community." Fowler recognized the board's limited
ability to manage population shifts and suggested: ". . . working with the
Knoxville Housing Authority and the Negro community to integrate
the housing projects better."[8]

New construction concerns were primarily those in the north (new
Central High School), west (new Bearden High School), and east (new
unnamed elementary) areas of the city. The plaintiffs contended that
these new facilities were located so as to continue segregation, or at least
not assist in desegregating the system.

Dr. Olin Adams Jr. and staff. (From left to right, standing): Dr. Earl Henry, Dr. Fred Bedelle Jr., and E. N. Aslinger; (seated): Ted Ballard, Superintendent Adams, and Dr. Roy Wallace. Photo courtesy of Fred Bedelle Jr.

However, the transfer provisions had always been challenged by the plaintiffs and would continue to present problems. Fowler was direct with the suggestion: ". . . the transfer rules should be changed to reduce the requests for transfer to a manageable load."

The letter ended with a paragraph containing the truism that had been with some members of the board all along and also made it plain where Fowler stood on the issue:

> We recognize that lately the opinion is being expressed that the 1954 integration decision of the Supreme Court will prove to be futile like the prohibition amendment to the Constitution. Even if this is true, we adhere to the above recommendations for a least two reasons: first, neither the courts nor HEW have adopted that view; second, if the two races actually can't be mixed 100%, we think that some degree of integration educationally will be of help to avoid future friction in this community.[9]

At the regular board meeting on March 9, 1970, Lynn Craig resigned as president of the board and immediately thereafter resigned his position as a member of the board. This action seemed to have taken the other board members by surprise. Craig had been re-elected for a second term but was elected as president of the board in a split vote of board members.

The *Knoxville Journal* reported: "At the first meeting in January the board chose Mr. Charles Burchett chairman by secret ballot. That same evening, however, the board held a second election and Craig was the winner."[10] Craig gave as his reason for resigning from the board: "I can no longer afford the personal time to serve and so I do resign."[11] After a little parliamentary maneuvering, Howard Temple was elected president (chairman) of the board.

This event graphically illustrated that the nine-member board had just as much division as the old five-member board when it came to desegregation. The political impact of district representation would become more evident in subsequent board discussions. Sarah Moore Greene consistently and skillfully represented the community that elected her.

A hearing was held on March 16, 1970, on the Motion for Immediate Relief and the Motion to Dismiss. Arguments were heard and taken under advisement by the court. Attorneys were given seven days to file briefs. The board filed answers to supplemental interrogatories on March 19. On March 27, attorneys filed briefs ordered by the March 16 hearing.

Judge Taylor denied the board's Motion to Dismiss on April 3. The order also addressed the plaintiffs' Motion for Immediate Relief and the matters to be argued at the upcoming hearing:

> Plaintiffs' motion as amended avers that defendant is operating a racially segregated school system by means of gerrymandering geographic school zone lines; building new schools or expanding existing facilities in neighborhoods which are predominantly black or white to perpetuate the existing segregated system; and assigning, hiring or discharging school personnel, including faculty, staff, administrative, maintenance and operational personnel in a manner designated to promote racial segregation.

Regarding school personnel, this Court stated that:

> "It was held in the case of *Mapp v. Board of Education of City of Chattanooga, Tennessee*, 319 F.2d 571 at 576 (C. A. 6), that

school personnel other than teachers and principals cannot be considered in a class action brought by students. The Court referred the case back to the District Court to consider faculty desegregation only. See *Bradley v. School Board of City of Richmond*, 382 U.S. 103, 86 S.Ct. 224, 15 L.Ed.2d 187. The present suit is a class action brought by students and parents and precludes consideration of school personnel other than faculty." *Goss v. Board of Education, City of Knoxville, Tennessee*, 270 F. Supp. 903, 914

This point was not reversed on appeal. Consequently, the Court will only consider evidence of discrimination in the hiring, assignment and discharge of principals and teachers since 1967. . . . The Court has not ruled upon the alleged gerrymandering of neighborhood zones since 1967 or the location of the above facilities which were built since 1967 allegedly to perpetuate a dual school system. These matters are not res judiciata, and therefore the Motion to Dismiss is overruled. . . .

In sum, in the hearing on the merits, the proof will be confined to the following matters: (1) whether the Board has practiced discrimination in the hiring, assignment, and discharge of principals and teachers since June 7, 1967; (2) whether the Board has engaged in gerrymandering of the neighborhood school zones since June 7, 1967; (3) and whether buildings at Bearden Junior High, Central High, West High and Agee Building, and an unnamed grammar school, planned after June 7, 1967, were constructed to perpetuate a dual school system.[12]

The *Knoxville News-Sentinel* reported: "School Mixing Hearing Ordered" and "City Must Show Compliance." Avon Williams argued that the system was not in compliance with Constitutional requirements because: "There are 18 secondary schools in the city, four schools had no integration or less than 1 percent. The other 14 have less than

5 percent integration . . ."[13] He would continue throughout the remaining years of this case to claim that every school should have a race mix of the students, faculty, and staff that reflected the race mix of the city of Knoxville as a whole.

On April 9, 1970, Sam Fowler included a paragraph in a billing statement to the board explaining the action, or reaction, to the plaintiffs' Motion for Immediate Relief:

> Plaintiffs filed a Motion for Immediate Relief which had the effect of asking that each school in the system immediately be restricted so that there are 15% to 20% Negroes in every school. We prepared a Motion to Dismiss on the ground that the court had already held that the system was integrated. A Brief was prepared and filed in support of the Motion. There was a hearing in Federal Court and both parties prepared and filed Supplemental Briefs. The Judge ruled that only teacher placement and new school construction could be litigated.[14]

The plaintiffs filed a motion on April 13 to alter or amend the order of April 3, 1970, or in the alternative, to certify and stay said Order for Appeal. The brief filed the same day asked the court to:

1. Order defendants to obtain the assistance of a competent desegregation expert and to submit to this Court within 30 days a comprehensive plan which will work realistically and now to dismantle the segregated school system in Knoxville, Tennessee, and provide desegregation in all aspects of all schools for all children, in said system. The plaintiffs will provide the Court with names of competent desegregation experts if requested.

2. Issue a preliminary injunction immediately restraining defendants from proceeding further with all new construction less than 40% complete at the time of the filing of the Motion for Immediate Relief or expansion or purchase of closure of old schools in the Knoxville School System

whether in the existing or planning stage, and whatever the stage, pending the submission of and hearing upon said plan to be filed by the defendants.

3. Proceed promptly to consider and approve the constitutional final plan for the operation of the public schools of the City of Knoxville, Tennessee, as a unitary school system, giving this matter the highest priority on the Court's docket.

4. Allow plaintiffs their costs, reasonable attorney fees and general relief.[15]

Fowler replied to the Motion to Amend on April 14. The first sentence of the reply set the tone for his argument against the motion: "This motion is a repetition of the Motion for Immediate Relief in all respects, except that it asks in the alternative for an appeal under 28 U.S.C. 1292(b)." He went on to argue: "The truth of the matter is as Mr. Williams observed in oral argument, the plaintiffs just do not like the *Deal* case [369 F. 2d 55 (6th Cir. 1966)] and its holding. Just because some schools are exclusively Negro does not prove by itself that the plaintiffs are being denied their constitutional rights."[16]

Fowler's argument must have been effective because on the same day it was filed, Judge Taylor issued orders that denied plaintiffs' Motion for Appeal and the Motion to Reconsider. As scheduled, a hearing was held on April 21. All evidence was heard and taken under advisement by the court. Attorneys were allowed thirty days to file briefs on conclusions of law and findings of fact.

Plaintiffs filed interrogatories on April 23, with a Motion for the Production of Documents for inspection, copying, and filing as evidence and interrogatories in the April 21, 1970, hearing record. Fowler filed objections to the Motion for the Production of Documents on May 4. He objected on the grounds that:

1. no records exist that showed the exact information desired,
2. that there was a distinct possibility that the information could not be retrieved from any source,

3. that the defendants were willing to open their records to plaintiffs but indicated that the procedures necessary to search out the desired information was a time-consuming process,

4. that the expense of answering interrogatories in this suit was a great financial burden,

5. that the request had come too late, and that the defendants objected to receiving the answers to these interrogatories into evidence without an opportunity to reopen the record and present any necessary rebuttal.[17]

On May 6, 1970, Fowler sent a letter to Superintendent Adams recalling the letter of February 24, 1970. Copies of this letter had been given to all board members, and "to date the board has taken no action." The letter had a synopsis of the *Swann* case. He pointed out that in 1965, the district court had found that system to be in compliance with the law, and this decision was upheld in the court of appeals. Then in 1969 the district court found: "They [the Charlotte-Mecklenberg School Board] have achieved a degree and volume of desegregation of schools apparently unsurpassed in these parts and may have exceeded the performance of any school board whose actions have been reviewed in the appellate court decisions." Fowler's letter ended with two paragraphs of significance:

> With all this going for them, they were still ordered prior to any hearing to transfer 5,000 inter-city black students to the suburbs and 5,000 whites to the inter-city when the school system did not have the buses to handle it.

> There are literally hundreds of school districts all over the South that are fighting for their very existence. Knoxville will be in the same situation unless the school board continues to exercise the imaginative initiative which it has exercised in the past. Up to now the school board has accepted our recommendations, and we have been fortunate enough to stay out of serious trouble. If the school board does not take more affirmative action to bring

about more racial mixing by September, 1970 the courts will bring about far more drastic changes. If you think you have problems now, you haven't seen anything yet.[18]

Judge Taylor issued an Order and Opinion of the Court on May 12, 1970, that the objections of the defendants to the interrogatories were well taken, but the defendants had offered to make the records available to the plaintiffs and the judge ordered:

the defendants to open their records to plaintiffs if plaintiffs wish to seek out this information; further ordered that defendants produce all teacher applications during the 1967, 1968, and 1969 terms for inspection and copying solely to plaintiffs' attorneys who will treat the information contained therein in a confidential manner; . . . plaintiffs motion to introduce evidence relating to interrogatories or motions to produce is denied.[19]

Fowler sent a letter to the superintendent's office on May 13. He explained the judge's order as follows:

Enclosed you will find an order which Judge Taylor entered in regard to the additional interrogatories. You will note that they can copy the records if they want to, but you don't have to answer the interrogatories.

The information in regard to the teachers will be kept confidential, and only the attorneys may see it. They may not use clerks or other type people to gather this type information, and it will be sealed and delivered to the court.[20]

An Agreed Order extending the time attorneys had to make findings of fact and conclusions of law and to file briefs, to and including June 10, was filed on May 20, 1970. Briefs were filed on June 10, and defendants filed a supplemental brief on June 23.

Judge Taylor issued a memorandum opinion on July 1, 1970. He ruled that the board was operating a unitary school system as defined by the Supreme Court in the case of *Alexander, Supra,* (396 U.S. 1218 [1969]) and the Motion for Relief was denied. The order was filed on July 22, 1970, and the case was taken off the docket, effective January 1971.[21] For a few years, Knoxville shared a designation ("unitary") that only two systems in the nation had been given. The other system was Orange County, Florida.[22]

Fowler followed this decision with a letter to the newly appointed superintendent, Elmer N. Aslinger, recounting a conversation with the staff member responsible for the desegregation activities of the board. This conversation involved several recommendations that Fowler had made. These recommendations had been discussed with the superintendent, and the superintendent had discussed them with members of the board.

The board was prepared to restructure the zones of Rule High School and Beardsley Junior High School to relieve some of the crowded situation at Rule and to bring Beardsley to near capacity. This zone change and grade structure change were made rather than pairing the two schools, because of distances involved. The ninth and tenth grades were to be dropped from Beardsley and all tenth, eleventh, and twelfth grade students would attend Rule.

Superintendent (1971–73) Elmer N. Aslinger. Photo courtesy of the Knox County Museum of Education.

The board proposed changing the transfer policy by eliminating the grade requirement and the brother-sister clauses and limiting hardship transfers to economic hardship. This change was deemed necessary in order to enforce the zone lines between Rule and Beardsley.

Fowler suggested that the board make formal the "majority-to-minority"

Superintendent Elmer N. Aslinger and staff. (From left to right, standing): Harry Gillespie, LeRoy Steinhoff, Dr. Funson Edwards, and Dr. Earl Henry; (seated): Dr. Fred Bedelle Jr., Superintendent Aslinger, Dr. Roy Wallace, and Ted Ballard. Photo courtesy of Fred Bedelle Jr.

transfer. This would let a white or black student attending a school where their race was in the majority to transfer to a school where their race was in the minority. This simply meant that no black students would be forced to attend a predominantly black school nor would it compel a white student to attend a predominantly white school.

Fowler also brought to the superintendent's attention the fact that Holston High School was overcrowded and if something was not done about that situation, the board should prepare a written explanation and submit it to the court. He also recommended that the board should have a biracial faculty and staff in every school, if at all possible, for the beginning of the 1971–72 school year.

The board immediately began considering these recommendations. As discussions proceeded, the zone changes and school reorganization began to receive opposition. The plan the board had decided on for Rule and Beardsley dropped the tenth grade from Beardsley, with these students attending Rule, and changed the zone line between Rule and Beardsley for all seventh graders. This change would have the effect of making Beardsley into the traditional junior high school, filling the school to capacity and adding students from Beardsley's tenth grade to Rule High School. The racial mixture would be increased in both schools.

The plan was adopted by a seven-to-one vote with one member absent. The one dissenting vote came from Kenneth Bailes, representing Rule/Beardsley district. The *Knoxville Journal* reported Bailes as

Mayor of Knoxville (1965–71) Leonard Rogers. Photo courtesy of City of Knoxville website, www.cityof knoxville.org/mayors.

saying: "I am opposed to transporting for racial balance, but this is even worse than busing for racial balance because we are not even offering buses."[23]

In consideration of the distances, lack of sidewalks, and the protests of a group of parents represented by counsel, the board indicated it would ask city council to provide sidewalks and public transportation for the areas concerned. Mayor Leonard Rogers, elected in 1965, was soon to respond with: "There are no funds available for either side-walks or transportation."[24]

In addition to the zone changes, the board restricted transfer requests to: (1) vocational or special education offerings, (2) administrative reassignment, (3) economic hardship, and (4) the majority-to-minority transfer.

The school year of 1970–71 opened with the new zones in place, as well as the new school organization for Beardsley and Rule, on a peaceful and relatively smooth basis. The principal of Rule reported that about forty parents tried to enroll their seventh grade children in Rule but were told they had to go to Beardsley. In order to accommodate the children who had been assigned to Beardsley, Knoxville Transit Authority decided to run a bus from the former Rule zone to Beardsley on a trial basis. The trial was successful enough to make the run permanent.

The actions taken by the board were more restrictive than former policies and were designed to comply with the court orders involving the decisions rendered in other desegregation cases in federal court circuits other than the Sixth Circuit. Regulations coming from the Office of Civil Rights and HEW were also getting into the mix of board concerns.

Knoxville was off the blackball list for eligibility for federal funds available for desegregation efforts. However, to receive any of this money, a school system had to meet certain requirements established by HEW. One regulation that surprised most systems was the requirement that the system had to "form a student biracial committee in each school affected by the project." The regulation was very specific about the makeup of the committee. "The number of minority and non-minority students serving on each such committee shall be equal."[25]

The desegregation money was limited; there were no guidelines to making applications. The deadline for making application was less than ten days from the time the board was notified that Knoxville was eligible. The superintendent's staff developed a project (staff development), and submitted the proposal, but it never materialized.

Avon Williams filed a Notice of Appeal for the plaintiffs on July 22, 1970, but asked for and received an order extending the time for docketing the appeal to ninety days. On September 29, a certified copy of the record was mailed to the clerk of the US Sixth Circuit Court of Appeals.

Additions and modifications to the desegregation plan required to comply with latest court decisions and HEW regulations continued to occupy efforts of the board. Community opposition to the actions was mounting.

The proposed site for the new elementary school in East Knoxville had become an issue. The *Knoxville News-Sentinel* reported that board member Kenneth Bailes called the proposed expenditure for the site "extravagant and wasteful spending."[26] The next day an article in the same newspaper indicated the price of the land had jumped $96,400 since the last appraisal. The board stayed with its decision and the land was purchased.

On June 14, 1971, Representative Robert Booker presented the board with a resolution naming the proposed school Sarah Moore Greene Elementary School. She was a sitting board member, and the board's policy was not to name a school after a living person. Discussion followed and when the vote was taken, it was a solid, but not uninamous, approval of the motion. Luther Woods passed and John Humphreys voted "no," saying: "I have nothing against Mrs.

Greene but think one Green School is enough."[27] Humphreys was referring to the Green Elementary School that existed long before this action.

A decision in *Bradley v. School District of The City of Richmond, Virginia* on April 5, 1971, gave the board and its counsel cause for concern. The decision was very specific and gave sweeping responsibility for execution and expected results. This opinion was written by US District Judge Robert R. Merhinge Jr. It ordered Richmond to consolidate with neighboring systems (Enrico and Chesterfield Counties) and bus students to school in such a fashion that each school would reflect the racial composition of the three systems combined. In order for the reader to understand the concern in Knoxville, the following excerpts are provided:

> The day is past when courts held that available injunctive relief did not encompass orders specifying the manner in which state officials might collect or disburse public funds. When taxing or spending powers have been used in such a manner as to infringe upon constitutional guaranties, and in cases when the exercise of such authority pursuant to judicial order is a form of relief "necessary to prevent further racial discrimination," . . . a federal court may govern by decree the discretion of state officers over the levying and diversion of public funds.

> . . . Although the entire effects of past illegal discrimination are beyond any court's power to alleviate, officials of the City of Richmond at least have made plans in order, to the extent feasible within their powers, to prevent further injury. In view of the defendants' demonstrated reluctance even now to provide the plaintiff class the full measure of their legal rights, an injunctive order requiring them to execute those plans promptly and effectively is entirely appropriate.

> An order shall enter directing the School Board and City Council of the City of Richmond and the City itself and all

others acting in concert with them forthwith to commence "all necessary clerical and administrative steps—such as determining new student assignments, bus routes and athletic schedules and preparing for any necessary physical changes— preparatory to complete conversion," under plan 3, such preparation to be completed in sufficient time to operate the city schools under that plan commencing the 1971–72 school year, and directing the same defendants "to take no steps which are inconsistent with, or which tend to prejudice or delay such preparation and operation."

The decree shall also oblige those defendants to acquire by purchase, lease or other contract those transportation facilities which are necessary in the judgment of the School Board to implement the student assignments ordered under plan 3. The evidence before the Court at this point is that a minimum of 56 buses will be needed. Further studies of routes and travel times, attempts to devise feasible schedules for study and extracurricular activities, and consideration of safety and disciplinary problems may persuade the School Board that they must have more than that number. If so, to ensure the successful operation of plan 3 it is their duty to acquire them, so far as necessary to this end, to divert funds budgeted for other uses.

At the same time all parties are cautioned that the operation of city schools free from racial bars may not be cause for a reduction in educational quality or the discontinuance of courses, services, programs, or extracurricular activities tradi- tionally offered. Those defendants who have such power will be directed, respectively to request and to raise and appropriate all funds requisite for the operation of the city school system in full compliance with the terms of this memorandum.

An appropriate Order will enter.[28]

The mayor and city council members were quoted as saying the city could not afford busing. However, as a defensive strategy, the assistant superintendent would present to the biracial committee and to the board a plan for busing large numbers of students in order that the public would be aware of the impact of busing on Knoxville. The board would be given many recommendations from the biracial committee, the superintendent's staff, citizens, and citizen groups, and counsel. All were intended to keep the unitary status that Judge Taylor had given the system and that the appeals court had upheld.

Faculty mixing began in 1965–66, but no formal policy had been established. Upon advice of counsel, the board considered what was referred to as "the Singleton Provision," which had resulted from the *Singleton v. Jackson School District* (419 F2d 1211) decision in 1970. This provision required that the faculty in each school should reflect the racial composition of the system as a whole with a 5 percent plus-or-minus variance. For Knoxville this meant that every school should have 10 to 20 percent black faculty members. The board also passed procedures (which were already in administrative practice), for accomplishing this policy:

1. The percentage race balance first attempted through replacement assignment.
2. Transfer requests which will facilitate the percentage race balance will be utilized.
3. As a last resort, administrative transfer to achieve the percentage race balance will be made by the Personnel Office.[29]

The Sixth Circuit Court of Appeals issued a decision on June 22, 1971, that denied plantiffs' appeal but kept the case on the docket. The case was remanded to the district court for further proceedings "consistent with *Swann v. Charlotte-Mecklenburg Bd. Of Ed.*, 402 U.S. 1, 91S.Ct. 1267, 28 L.Ed.2d 554, and other relevant Supreme Court opinions announced on April 20, 1971."[30]

In response to the decision rendered by the court of appeals on June 22, 1971, and before the district court held a hearing to carry out the appeals court decision, the superintendent's staff devised and prepared a pupil locator map that identified every student in the system by race and by residence.

The map divided the city into one-thousand-foot grids. Each grid square could be located by a vertical number and a horizontal letter. Personnel in every school found the address of each student and the grid in which that address fell. The student's name, race, and grid number were listed and sent to the superintendent's office. A designated staff member placed the student in the appropriate grid and color coded every grid as to the percentage of black and white students in each grid. It was done manually and took hours and hours of tedious work.[31]

On July 1, Judge Taylor issued a memorandum opinion that the "defendant school board is operating a unitary school system as defined by the Supreme Court in the case of *Alexander, Supra,* and the Motion for Immediate Relief in the form of an injunction must be denied."[32]

On July 6, plaintiffs filed a motion to require defendants "forthwith to prepare, file with the court and furnish the plaintiffs copy of pupil locator map."[33] Three days later, Judge Taylor denied the plaintiffs' motion to require the defendants to furnish plaintiffs a copy of the pupil locator map, except the defendants are "required and directed to make available to plaintiffs records from which information sought may be derived and afford plaintiffs reasonable opportunity to examine, audit and inspect such records and to make copies . . ." The board was directed to complete the pupil locator map within a reasonable time. On the same day, the court issued a notice of pre-trial conference and set the date for the trial on the merits of the case for September 7, 1971.[34]

The idea of a biracial committee to advise the board was presented by attorney Fowler, with nominations coming from several organizations throughout the city. In executive session on July 26, 1971, the board formed and approved a fifteen-member committee composed of seven black and eight white members. The individuals selected for the original committee were: Rev. R. E. James, Eloise Dupree, Dr. Howard Senter, Horace Anderson, James R. Rowan Jr., Tommy Moore, Joyce Williams, Howard Bozeman, Fred Comer, Lewis Van Mol, Herbert

Waters, Fred McPeake, Rev. Charles Trentham, Nancy J. (Mrs. Tom) Siler, and Dr. Don Dessart. Ten other individuals were selected as alternates: Oscar White, Sammy Coleman, Rev. R. E. Anderson, Wallace Frazier, Will Tom Moore, Bob Ray, John Massey, Joe Toliver, Bill Padgett, and Robert Wynn. Howard Bozeman, county judge, was appointed chairman.

This committee and members thereof were approved at the regular meeting of the board on August 4, 1971. The *Knoxville News-Sentinel* carried the headline: "Desegregation Advisors Named."[35]

The biracial committee members would begin their work with a confused idea of their mission. Through the rigors of sorting out the various plans and the community reactions to these plans, the mission would be defined in short order. It became a very important communication tool for the board since the black community, in general, had very little confidence in its actions.

The 1964 Civil Rights Act was being administered more vigorously by HEW, which almost daily handed down more regulations and descriptions of what a system had to do in developing its desegregation plan.

The Sixth Circuit Court of Appeals had ordered the district court to determine if the Knoxville Board of Education's plan met the criteria of the *Swann* decision. The *Singleton v. Jackson Municipal Separate School District* (419 F. 2d 1211) required teachers to be hired, assigned, promoted, paid, demoted, dismissed, and otherwise treated without regard to race, or national origin. And if there had to be a staff reduction, it would affect black and white teachers equally. The *Montgomery County Board of Education v. US Supreme Court* (395 U.S. 225 [1969]) required the ratio of white teachers and black teachers to approach the total racial ratio of teachers in the entire district. Both of these were included in the *Swann* decision.

The board had to modify the Knoxville plan to meet the requirements of HEW and court at the same time, and adjust to the appointment of a new superintendent, Dr. Roy W. Wallace. The board acted more vigorously on HEW requirements because money to operate various programs was at stake, and as a practical matter, regulations from the state and federal authorities did not require board approval in many cases. The superintendent's staff initiated many changes just as a matter of normal operation.

The biracial committee held its organizational meeting on August 5, 1971, and immediately began to discuss how to increase the race mix in all the schools. Sam Fowler suggested that the committee consider ways to reduce the black population in all predominantly black schools to less than 50 percent of the student body. He was of the opinion that it might be possible by rezoning, but some transportation might be necessary. The headline of the article in the *Knoxville News-Sentinel* August 6, 1971 read: "Bi-racial Group Dislikes Busing."

In addition to the committee formed by the board, other community groups were forming to collectively present their views. As the board amended the desegregation plan to comply with the changing court decisions and regulations from HEW, these other community groups became more vocal.

The biracial committee became a sounding board for the external groups to make their recommendations. The volume of requests and demands became a divisive situation with each group thinking of their individual school and making recommendations that would apply to their school but not necessarily the whole system.

Pressure from court decisions outside the Sixth Circuit requiring cross-district busing to achieve certain racial percentages in each school was beginning to concern the board and their attorney.

The communities, white and black, were now resisting the busing solution. The mixing of the faculties on the ratio of blacks to whites in the community was devastating to the predominantly

Superintendent (1973–75) Dr. Roy W. Wallace.
Photo courtesy of Knox County Museum of Education.

Dr. Roy Wallace and staff. (From left to right, standing): Harry Gillespie, Dr. Paul Kelley, LeRoy Steinhoff, and Earl Henry; (seated): George Whedbee, Superintendent Wallace, Dr. Fred Bedelle Jr., and Wanda Moody. Photo courtesy of Fred Bedelle Jr.

black faculties, but did little to disturb the all-white faculties. Communities were now raising the question: "Why?"

The month of August 1971 was a month of intensive activity. On August 5 the so-called "lottery" to finally mix all the faculties was held. At that time all teachers available for the high school faculty mix were already assigned. The junior high faculties were within less than twenty-five positions of being within the desired ratio. Of the city's 47 elementary schools, 17 had the proper ratio, 18 were within one teacher, 6 schools were within two positions, 3 schools needed three positions, and 3 schools needed several assignments.

As the effort proceeded, most of these situations were solved without using the lottery selections. However, Sam Hill, Maynard, and Eastport Elementary Schools were problems that did not get corrected in 1971, but would take another two years to approach the desired ratio.

At the regular meeting on August 9, 1971, the board revised the student transfer policy to allow transfers out of assigned zones only for the majority-to-minority transfer, vocational course offerings, special education programs, and preschool programs operated by the board.

George B. Smith, president of the predominately black Austin-East High School's PTA, appeared before the board at this meeting to question why the board was transferring a majority of the black teachers out of A-E and replacing them with white faculty. He said: "The situation is already tense, and this isn't going to make it any better. Black people are tired of getting things stuffed down their throats."[36]

The educational effects of removing a majority of black teachers from Austin-East (or any black school) and assigning them to predominatly white faculties was detrimental to both the receiving school as well as the school from which they came. Effective teachers, long-standing residents of the community who knew most of the students, were exchanged for young white teachers from outside the community. Leadership and continuity of instructional elements of departments were damaged by the loss of the experienced teachers. Discipline became a major problem.

Additional efforts by the board during the 1971 summer to comply with the provisions of *Swann* were:

1. Authorized the creation and maintenance of a pupil locator map;
2. Established a policy of assigning faculty and supporting staff, insofar as is administratively sound, to have the faculty of each school reflect the racial balance of the school system as a whole;
3. Required all transfers to be renewed annually and would be honored only as long as the original basis remained valid;
4. Made the following zone adjustments:
    (a) Pair Sam Hill and Lonsdale Elementary Schools;
    (b) Move the severely mentally retarded program at Beaumont and the preschool program at Moses to Cansler; and close the regular program at Cansler by dividing its regular pupils between Beaumont and West View;
    (c) Move the regular program at Moses to Maynard and expand the special education program at Moses;
    (d) Organized Beardsley as a two-year junior high and Rule as a four year senior high serving the present Rule-Beardsley attendance zones;
    (e) Moved the Austin-East zone line further east;
    (f) Paired the vocational programs at Austin-East and Fulton;
    (g) Assured the election of minority race cheerleaders.[37]

These actions were taken after receiving recommendations from the biracial committee, members of the community, and members of the school staffs in an effort to avoid the court requiring busing to increase the racial mix of students.

The desegregation plan adopted by the board earlier had been revised again in an attempt to increase the racial mix of students and to keep the neighborhood school concept. The *Knoxville News-Sentinel* reported the changes as: "Knox School Plan Ready for Court," saying, "The Knoxville Board of Education will present a Desegregation plan to Federal Court Sept. 7 that is little changed from last year's and leaves some schools basically all Negro or all white in student population." It further stated: ". . . the Assistant Superintendent for Personnel and Development said the plan, 'was drawn up with the idea to do what we can without busing to achieve desegregation.'"[38]

The *Knoxville Journal* carried a headline: "Duncan Says He Opposes Busing To Achieve Intergation In Schools." Congressman Duncan's reasons had to do with the limited finances of the city and the former Knoxville mayor was of the opinion that: "Most of the black families are against busing."[39]

The neighborhood school concept had been the backbone of the board's position throughout the life of the litigation. At this point, however, decisions in jurisdictions outside the Sixth Circuit and similar cases, that had a completely different body of facts and circumstances, were causing the board concern.

Whereas some boards had resisted desegregation until a judge ordered it and outlined what that board must do, the Knoxville Board of Education had taken the position that: "We will do our constitutional duty with as little disruption to the schools as possible and as our duties are determined."[40] This position kept the board in a cooperative relationship with the court and never forced Judge Taylor to ask HEW for assistance.

Although the plaintiffs would keep insisting that the actions of the board had not done away with the dual system and continued to ask the judge to order the board to ask HEW for assistance, Judge Taylor never acted as though he thought the board was refusing to desegregate the schools without a direct order.

The original plan the court had approved was modified voluntarily, although reluctantly on occasion, as it became evident to Sam Fowler that court decisions in other cases would in fact be applied to the *Goss* case.

The *Knoxville News-Sentinel* reported on a meeting of an East Knoxville citizens group that had organized to set up defenses in case the board adopted amendments to the desegregation plan they thought to be discriminatory to their schools. One group consisted of about one hundred residents from the Holston-Chilhowee communities without any blacks in attendance. The meeting concerned the rezoning the board had been discussing which would have moved the Austin-East zone further east, forcing some whites to go to Austin-East instead of Holston High.[41]

The plaintiffs would continue to insist that the system was not unitary because it still had some predominately black schools and white schools that were the same under the dual system, that *Swann* required a mixing in every school, and busing should be ordered if necessary to achieve some percentage of race mixing in each school.

The busing issue began to draw national attention involving Southern congressmen and some Northern congressmen as the courts and HEW began to look at some of the segregated systems (in the North) not resulting from de jure segregation. North Carolina's Senator Sam Ervin Jr. proposed a law to curb the powers of the appeals courts. As emotions grew regarding busing in the North and South for the purpose of integregation in schools, the bill gained support. At one point, only six votes were needed to pass the bill, and the president would probably have signed it.

The remainder of August 1971 was used by the biracial committee and the board to explore several avenues to further desegregation before the case came up for trial again in September. "White flight" was beginning to defeat almost any arrangements the board could plan in the East area. On September 7, an injunction was requested to keep the city students from attending a county school. It was turned down. Avon Williams said that he had been told that approximately three hundred students were planning to transfer from the Holston attendance zone to the county.[42] The *Knoxville News-Sentinel* published a story headlined: "School Planners Race with Time: Mixing Blueprint Needed by Sept. 1."[43] This article indicated that the biracial committee had voted to meet three times during the week of August 17 "to help the board to get ready."

Fowler was concerned that the *Swann* decision would make it difficult for Judge Taylor to accept any plan that would leave any school with an all-black student body. There was also the situation that the scheduling of the trial for September 7 would mean that any court decision ordering the movement of students would require moving students after school had started.

The emotional objection to desegregation had been underplayed during the early years of this case and the *Brown* decision, mainly because the board had chosen the least disruptive route to desegregation. The district court had approved the board's plan as it was modified to reflect the different definitions of "desegregated" school systems. The upcoming hearing would compare the progress Knoxville had made to the decisions reached in other cases throughout the South and, in particular, the *Swann* decision.

Busing was the foremost issue for the September hearing. The biracial committee met on three consecutive evenings as planned. At each meeting a member of the superintendent's staff presented a plan that would desegregate the schools to a greater degree. Plans ranged from minimal changes to complete busing.

On August 18, 1971, the *Knoxville News-Sentinel* reported that "East Knoxville Group Opposes Changes." The article said that both Negroes and whites expressed similar opinions on keeping the schools the same as they were during the past school year, but for different reasons. Kenneth Gresham, a member of the community, said a system of pairing schools in the East Knoxville area to achieve racial balance would result in all schools becoming predominately black in a short while. Stanley Scandrick, a recent graduate of Austin-East High, said the people in his community wanted all the schools that had a predominantly Negro enrollment "to remain black. The black community does not want integration. It is not the answer to the black man's problem because it will put chains back on him."[44]

At the committee meeting held on the following night, the board's representative presented another plan. This plan suggested pairing schools, changing grade levels in schools, adjusting attendance zones, and altering programs. A second plan was presented by an East Knoxville group. A newspaper account stated: "Several of the 40 persons at the meeting expressed the opinion that the school board was only going to come up with a solution that will satisfy the courts and not one that will benefit the city on a long-range basis."[45]

Community impatience and frustration was evident. Police Lt. Jim Rowan, a black committee member, said: "Under the new proposed plan, Austin-East would revert to a nearly all-black school because within five years all the white residents north of Magnolia Avenue will move out." Jim Kincaid, a black University of Tennessee student, also expressed the opinion that the whole plan would deteriorate in five years. He said the school board seemed interested in "doing the very least they can get by with to get the heat off, rather than creating a viable social system we can all live in."[46]

Avon W. Rollins, a Tennessee Valley Authority (TVA) employee and civil rights activist, said the biracial committee should make suggestions to the city and county governments on issues of fair housing and equal job opportunities for Negroes.

With elections of some board members coming up in November, there were some political concerns. The board issued a statement to the biracial committee which was read by committee member Fred Comer:

> The board will do everything in its power to comply with the requirements of the Constitution and the Supreme Court decisions.
>
> The board will endeavor to avoid forced extensive cross-city busing.

Avon W. Rollins is the current CEO of the Beck Cultural Exchange Center and was active in the civil rights movement in the South. He presented a desegregation plan to the advisory committee set up by the board of education that, if adopted, might have shortened the Goss *case by several years.* Photo courtesy of Fred Bedelle Jr.

The board will strive diligently to present a workable plan for further integrating the Knoxville city schools to the satisfaction of the courts with the least disruption to the school program.

It is the intent of the board to establish a plan that will be most acceptable to the greatest number of people.

The meeting of the biracial committee on August 19 was even more emotional. An appointed staff member described a complete busing scheme designed to produce the race mix that the plaintiffs had suggested. It also centered around moving the students from the East Knoxville area. Several proposals were made, with a majority opposing cross-system busing. Some of the people attending the meeting wore "black power" badges. Racial stress was becoming evident in several neighborhoods.[47]

Avon W. Rollins presented a plan on August 23 that many of the members of the biracial committee appeared to like as a possible alternative. This plan developed by a "group of concerned citizens" recommended: (1) that the school system stay as it is, with the transfer and zoning regulations being strictly enforced; (2) that the teacher ratio reflect the student ratio in each school; (3) emphasis be put on upgrading the quality of education in predominantly black schools through allocation of needed funds. Mr. Rollins said the group opposed any form of mass busing or any change to the grade level status of Austin-East High School.[48]

The board, as well as most of the white citizens of Knoxville, was unaware of the pride and ownership the black community held for the former Austin High School and Vine Junior High School. There was lingering resentment about the way Austin High had been discontinued and of the attempt to replace it with a white high school (East High). Although Austin-East High School was by now mostly black, the community did not want to entertain any thoughts of making it a junior high or anything else that would completely do away with any reference to Austin High School or Vine Junior High School. One of the plans presented to the biracial committee would have made A-E a junior high and moved the high school students to Holston High School. Rollins's proposal dealt with that idea directly.

Although the plan Rollins proposed would not fit directly into the orders of the court, it did express the reality of the situation. Without massive busing, it would get the focus back to improving the program for all students and off the mechanics of "the plan." It would also make the faculty mix more realistic in terms of the teachers available. More important, the community would support it.

On August 28, 1971, the *Knoxville News-Sentinel* carried an article with the caption: "Knox School Plan Ready for Court." There were minimal changes from the last plan submitted to and approved by the court. This plan would not involve any busing and would still leave some schools' student body all black and some all white. However, all faculties and staffs were desegregated. (See appendix E.)

The attorneys used August to file statements for the pre-trial conference, exceptions to the pre-trial order, and other legal maneuvering prior to the trial date.

On September 1, the board filed the amended desegregation plan adopted in August. On September 3, 1971, the board filed a motion to reset the trial from September 7, to a later date when the pupil locator map could be finished. Judge Taylor signed an Agreed Order setting the date for trial on the merits for October 21, 1971. He also issued an order that both parties file proposed findings of fact and conclusions of law, with supporting briefs, at least ten days before the trial date, and that the parties exchange names and addresses of witnesses on or before October 5, 1971.

On October 16, plaintiffs filed a motion to reset the case for hearing during the month of November. Judge Taylor set the trial date for December 1. The trial lasted for three days (December 1–3, 1971) with the main element of the plaintiffs' argument being that the system was not yet unitary because there were still black schools and white schools, and they wanted city council added as defendants in the case.

An Order for Joinder of Additional Parties was issued on December 6, and a Show Cause hearing was set for December 15. The show cause hearing was held and the plaintiffs prevailed. Knoxville City Council was added as defendants in the *Goss* case.

Theotis Robinson Jr., by this time a member of city council, was now both a plaintiff and defendant. (However, he was never summoned as a defendant.) The City of Knoxville was given additional time within which to prepare its defense. The case was postponed to January 31, 1972. W. P. Boone Dougherty joined Sam Fowler, the board's attorney, as counsel for the Knoxville City Council.

CHAPTER 6

UNITARY AT LAST

THE YEAR 1972 WOULD BRING THE *Goss* case into the final stage. Community frustration and anxiety with the changes the board was making began to be evident at board meetings and community gatherings. Threats to board members and some staff members, along with very disruptive actions at board meetings, would become frequent and serious.

As recap, here are the significant events and actions taken by the board that were directly connected with desegregation of the school system:

1954
- *Brown v. Topeka Board of Education* (*Brown I*)
- Rev. Frank Gordon asked board to desegregate immediately.

1955
- *Brown v. Topeka Board of Education* (*Brown II*).
- Thomas N. Johnston hired as superintendent of Knoxville city schools.
- Board instructed superintendent to develop a desegregation plan.

1956
- Clinton, Tennessee schools ordered to desegregate. (Judge Taylor's decision in *McSwain* case.)
- Board asked for more time to develop plan.

- Black students attempted to enroll in Staub, Mt. View, and East High.

1957
- *Dianne Ward et al. v. The Board of Education of the City of Knoxville, Tennessee, et al.*
- Three new members elected to school board.

1958
- S. Frank Fowler hired as legal counsel for board.
- Motion by board to dismiss *Ward* case.

1959
- *Ward* case dismissed on a technicality "without prejudice."
- *Josephine Goss et al. v. The Board of Education of the City of Knoxville, Tennessee, et al.*

1960
- S. Frank Fowler hired as legal counsel in *Goss* case.
- Adopted grade-a-year desegregation plan.
- Grade-a-year plan approved by Judge Taylor.
- First grade desegregated.

1961
- Vocational program set up for blacks similar to program for whites.
- Judge Taylor approved vocational plan except for Fulton High School.
- Board amended plan and Judge Taylor approved the amended plan.
- Case taken off the docket.
- Plaintiffs filed appeal with US Court of Appeals, Sixth Circuit.

1962
- US Court of Appeals approved plan except for Fulton High vocational program.
- Appeals court suggested speeding up desegregation plan, and instructed district court to keep case on docket.
- Board accelerated grade-a-year plan to include grades three and four.
- Grades one through four desegregated.

1963
- Annexation of eighteen schools and fifty-six square miles of territory.
- Desegregated grades one through six.
- Desegregated summer schools.
- US Supreme Court ruled transfer policy invalid.
- Distributive education and Van Gilder programs desegregated.
- Judge Taylor approved amended plan and ruled system unitary.
- Plaintiffs appealed decision to US Court of Appeals, Sixth Circuit.

1964
- Civil Rights Act became effective.
- US Court of Appeals, Sixth Circuit dismissed plaintiffs' appeal of June 7, 1963.
- Board approved plan for complete desegregation.
- Closed three black schools.
- Dr. Olin L. Adams Jr. hired as superintendent of Knoxville city schools.
- All grades, programs, and facilities desegregated.

1965
- Revised integration plan to comply with court required change.
- Began to mix faculties.
- Transfer policies made more restrictive.
- HEW and Office of Civil Rights issued desegregation regulations.
- Free summer schools.

1966
- Adopted brother-sister transfer policy.

1967
- Sam F. Fowler Jr. assumed major defense role from his father, S. Frank Fowler Sr.
- Held three-day trial.

- Judge Taylor denied plaintiffs' request and declared system "fully integrated."
- Ordered the case "off the docket."
- Decision appealed to US Court of Appeals, Sixth Circuit.

1968
- Closed Austin High School.
- Created Austin-East High School.

1969
- US Court of Appeals affirmed district court's 1967 decision, but kept case on the docket.
- US Supreme Court's decision in Mississippi case; "Integrate Schools at Once."
- Sarah Moore Greene elected to school board.
- Theotis Robinson Jr. elected to city council.
- *Swann v. Charlotte-Mecklenburg Board of Education* decision

1970
- Sam F. Fowler filed Motion to Dismiss.
- Board made Beardsley a seventh- and eighth-grade junior high school.
- Paired Sam Hill and Lonsdale schools.
- Motion to Dismiss denied.
- Trial held; case taken under advisement.
- Judge Taylor ruled board was operating a unitary school system.
- Case taken off the docket.
- Majority-to-minority transfer formalized.
- New elementary school named Sarah Moore Greene Elementary.
- Developed pupil locator map system.

1971
- Judge Taylor again ruled board was operating a unitary system.
- Elmer N. Aslinger hired as superintendent of Knoxville city schools.

- Completed faculty mixing.
- Developed biracial committee.
- Filed amended desegregation plan.
- Three-day trial held.
- City council added as defendants.
- Case postponed until 1972.

This summary covers the years of the major changes in school operations since the *Brown* decision. Three superintendents, annexation of eighteen schools, change in the structure of the board, and the different election process for both city council and the board of education made administration of the school system a difficult process.

Until 1972 the major changes had primarily involved East Knoxville schools and attendance zones. Significant changes in the Beaumont, Lonsdale, and Rule areas would produce heated exchanges between community members, the board, superintendent, and some staff members. As some of the plans included reorganization of grade levels in certain schools, the communities of each school became vocal in opposition to the changes.

The plaintiffs were focusing on the requirements of the *Swann* decision to require busing if the proper ratio of blacks and whites was to be required and maintained. The fact that Knoxville still had some all-white schools and some all-black schools, as they were under de jure segregation, was the basis for the plaintiffs' argument that Knoxville had not desegregated the system.

Boone Dougherty filed an answer to the Order for Joinder on January 20, 1972. His answer was simply based on the position of the Knoxville City Council at this time. New members had just been elected: Don Ferguson, M. T. Bellah, Arthur Blanchard, and Henry Ellenberg. An additional member, Gene Cathey, was appointed to replace Kyle Testerman, who had just been elected mayor. Very few members of that council remember even discussing their role in the lawsuit.

Dougherty's answer was:

1. The City of Knoxville is a municipal corporation and instrument of the State and is not subject to suit in this action by

virtue of the Eleventh Amendment to the Constitution of the United States.

2. These defendants are insufficiently advised concerning whether their absence as parties would prevent complete relief among those already parties.

3. These defendants admit that the City of Knoxville holds title to the property of the City of Knoxville public schools.

4. It is further admitted that the City Council approves all budgets and appropriates certain portions of the funds necessary to operate said school system. It must be pointed out that the City Council does not appropriate all of the funds necessary to operate said school system. Certain of these funds come from sources other than the City of Knoxville.

5. It is admitted that Mayor Kyle Testerman is the chief executive and administrative officer of the general government and prepares and submits the annual city budget.

6. It is admitted that former Mayor Leonard Rogers and present Mayor Kyle Testerman testified in this cause, stating in substance that there were no funds available in the budget to provide additional public school transportation.

7. It is denied that any order of this Court would in any way be hindered or deterred in its implementation by the Mayor or Council of the City of Knoxville.

8. These defendants aver that the City of Knoxville has a unitary school system and that having such, additional public school transportation and facilities are unnecessary.

9. This action should be dismissed.

10. These defendants aver that the City of Knoxville has a unitary public school system, and further, it does not contain vestiges of state imposed segregation.[1]

The plaintiffs responded on January 31, 1972, by denying all claims made by attorney Dougherty. Avon Williams ended his replication with:

All other averments of said Answer which raise affirmative
issues of fact or law in conflict with the pleadings heretofore
filed by plaintiffs in this case are generally denied.[2]

The board took the position that the concentration of blacks in
certain areas was not caused or controlled by the board; that all the
grades, programs, and facilities had been desegregated since 1964; that
Urban Renewal projects, highway construction, and annexation had
caused population shifts over which the board had no control, but
provided the board with zoning opportunities to mix more student
bodies; that the majority-to-minority transfer policy allows black or
white students to attend a school where their race is in the minority (no
student was locked into his/her situation because of race); and that the
board would continue to do everything possible to mix the races to a
greater percentage. However, busing was out of the question!

The hearing was held as scheduled on January 31, 1972, and lasted
four days, through February 3, 1972. The board presented the amended
plan that had been adopted in August 1971. On the first day of the trial,
Fowler began his defense against busing with witness Dr. Ernest Farmer,
director of transportation for the Tennessee Department of Education.
Farmer testified that state money for transportation would not be
available to the city the first year. Transportation monies were calculated
on the previous year's average daily attendance of students bused. It had
been established earlier that the city and county would have to enlarge
the annexation agreement if any funds were to come from the state. [3]

H. T. Ballard, assistant superintendent for finance, the next witness
for the defense, testified that the schools were looking at a budget deficit
because of the loss of approximately one thousand students who were
attending private, parochial, or county schools. He indicated that the
number of school personnel would have to be reduced to cover the loss.[4]

W. C. Walkup, president of Home Federal Savings and Loan,
testified that it had been a long-standing policy that his organization
loaned money to anyone who could qualify, regardless of race. Walkup
and attorney Williams got into a heated exchange when Williams

Mayor of Knoxville (1972–75 and 1984–87) Kyle C. Testerman. Photo courtesy of City of Knoxville website, www.cityof knoxville.org/mayors.

asked Walkup the same question over and over. Walkup answered: "You have asked me four times and I am going to give you the same answer four times in a row." He proceeded to repeat the answer four times.[5]

Mayor Kyle Testerman was the only defense witness on behalf of himself and the eight city council members added to the suit. He testified that any monies spent for busing would have to come from monies taken from other city needs and services. On cross-examination he was asked if the city could borrow the money for busing. His reply was, "No, because we have no source of revenue."[6]

Williams called John R. Goss, brother to Josephine Goss, to testify regarding moving his children from Fair Garden Elementary to Chilhowee Elementary. Goss testified that he moved his children in order that they would be afforded a better education. He said that it was a two-mile bus ride on a Knoxville Transit Lines bus at a cost of forty cents a day for each child. He also testified that he had gotten a vague answer from the school administration when he asked for the board to pay for the bus fares.

Judge Taylor asked Fowler if the board would provide transportation for students who transferred on the majority-to-minority transfer. He further asked: "Do you have any objection to the court ordering the board to pay for such transportation? If black students want to go to another school where they feel they can get a better quality education, don't you think they should?" Fowler answered that he did not know how much it would cost, but would have an answer by the end of the day.

Although Fowler did not give the answer until the afternoon session of court, the decision was made in the courtroom before Fowler returned to his seat. The assistant superintendent who was seated with

Fowler realized that Judge Taylor had expressed what he thought should happen, so he privately told Fowler: "The answer is yes." As soon as a recess was called, the superintendent was notified of the decision. The superintendent immediately scurried to secure board approval by phone. By the time Fowler delivered the decision to Judge Taylor, the board had actually approved providing transportation for the majority-to-minority transfers.

Transportation was an element that the board had only discussed as it developed the majority-to-minority transfer. Fowler later explained: "The majority-to-minority transfer was designed to make sure that no child was locked into school where his race was in the majority and wanted out. However, an argument could be made that a lot of black kids could not afford transportation to another school. This action takes away that argument!"

Plaintiffs alleged, and presented evidence, that the board had not established a unitary system because some schools were mostly white and some schools were mostly black, the building of new or refurbished school facilities continued segregation, and that the predominately black schools were inferior and used inferior materials as compared to white schools. The main point of the argument was that the only way to desegregate the system would be to bus students from one neighborhood to a school in another neighborhood.

Williams presented as his first witness, Martin E. Sloane, the acting deputy and staff director of the US Commission on Civil Rights. Sloane testified that "the Federal Housing Administration down through the years is the cause of many of the housing patterns that exist today." He went on to label the FHA as the "Typhoid Mary" of restrictive covenants. He indicated that although the practices of discrimination had been eliminated on paper, they had tended to go underground. Most of the testimony given by Sloane came from studies made by federal agencies, causing Judge Taylor to admonish Williams "to apply testimony to Tennessee and to Knoxville and to try to confine testimony to reality and not theory."

Plaintiffs' expert witnesses, Sloane, and Dr. Michael Stolee, presented themselves as experts in desegregation activities and plans in other school systems throughout the South. Their testimony was based on those situations in which they had direct contact and involvement and on results of studies they knew about. However, they were not very familiar with Knoxville's demographics or topography and testified from data provided them by plaintiffs' attorneys. This data had been subpoenaed from the defendants and provided by the superintendent's staff.

Williams called Stolee to the stand to explain his plan of desegregation for the Knoxville school system. Stolee testified that he had been given a copy of the printouts of data used to develop the pupil locator map, but did not use it. He said the reason he did not use that data was that it did not include those county students attending city schools.

On the elementary level, Stolee left six schools as they were. They met his desegregation test. The remaining elementary schools were divided into seven groups or clusters. Each cluster included one school with a majority black student body. Some of the clusters had schools with contiguous zones. Other clusters contained school zones that were noncontiguous.

Each cluster also had one school designated as a "grade center" serving a grade level for the entire cluster. Students living outside the zone designated for the grade center would be bused into the center. Those students living in the zone of the school designated as the center, but not in that grade, would be bused to other schools in the cluster.

Stolee estimated that the plan would require transporting approximately 75 percent of the elementary students in the system. These students would be attending a school outside their neighborhood. They would also be bused from one to six miles. Dr. Stolee's mileage estimates were calculated without developing bus routes, and thus, were determined to be significantly in error.

Major rearrangements of the structure of the grades contained in the junior high schools and high schools were proposed in Stolee's plan. The most drastic element involved South High School and Young High School, both of which contained grades seven through twelve. Stolee recommended that these schools be converted to grades nine through twelve senior high schools. The seventh and eighth grades of both schools would be bused to Vine Junior High School.

This one recommendation required that fourteen hundred children be bused in twenty-four sixty-passenger buses across the Henley Bridge twice a day. Other parts of the plan required another fourteen sixty-passenger buses carrying elementary students across the same bridge. The timing of the routes would be during morning and evening rush hours and through the business district of Knoxville.[7]

In cross examination, Fowler did not challenge the expertise of the witnesses, but brought out in great detail the flaws in their recommendations as affected by local terrain, traffic patterns, infrastructure (such as the few bridges across the river), and distances between schools. The pupil locator map system prepared by the board showed graphically that although the black population was concentrated in two locations, there was some race mixing in many of the schools. Enrollment data was presented that indicated that race mixing was increasing annually.

Williams called Councilman Theotis Robinson Jr., one of the original plaintiffs in the suit, to answer questions about the fiscal concerns relating to $1.5 million that could be made available from the city budget for busing. Robinson indicated that this amount had been set aside to pay off short-term notes that had been used for teacher raises. He also stated: "Integrated schools are necessary to guarantee quality education."[8]

Knox County Superintendent of Schools Mildred E. Doyle was called to testify regarding the availability of transportation. Superintendent Doyle testified that the county provided transportation for seven thousand city school students living in the annexed area. Fowler asked if the county would provide transportation for racial purposes. Her response was: "That would have to be a board decision."[9]

Witnesses from the various real estate organizations, financial institutions, housing authority, and the Metropolitan Planning Commission all had testified that they were operating according to legal requirements for each of their organizations and that no one was denied access to housing wherever they wanted and were qualified to purchase.

The racial composition of the various neighborhoods was the result of discrimination, according to the plaintiffs' witnesses, but no specific data was presented to prove the statement, except census data. This data only gave the race of people living in each district, but not the reason they were there.

The board had hired Dr. Charles Trotter, a professor in the University of Tennessee's College of Education, Department of Plant and Facilities Planning, to develop a plan of zoning, school organization, and pairing that would produce the greatest amount of race mixing without busing. This plan was approved by the board with two exceptions. Those exceptions were made because of the distances that students would have to walk to get to the schools assigned and the minimal impact it would have on the race composition in each school.

Trotter presented his plan as opposed to the plan presented by Stolee, the plaintiffs' expert. Fowler also presented evidence of mixing faculties and staffs, the openness provided by the majority-to-minority transfer provision, and the availability of programs.

The assistant superintendent presented the results of the pupil locator map and explained its function and how the board used the data to determine appropriate attendance zone lines for loading the schools. He also testified regarding the various changes made to produce the "final plan" the board had developed and adopted since the last hearing. Fowler used this staff member to explain the problems that Stolee's plan would produce. The staff member was vigorously cross-examined by Williams for more than eight hours.

On February 3, 1972, Judge Taylor took the case under advisement and gave each of the parties twenty days to submit final briefs.

Fowler filed a supplemental trial brief on behalf of the board on February 23. Dougherty filed a trial brief on behalf of the city council the same day in support of the brief filed by Fowler. Dougherty's brief stated:

> The General Government defendants respectfully submit that the supplemental trial brief filed by the defendant Board of Education very ably and thoroughly discusses and analyzes the issues presented in this cause, and accordingly adopt same.[10]

Fowler's brief went into detail regarding the board's position on the issues that would be important in finalizing the case. He started his brief with the statement:

> The *Swann* case makes it clear that the objective of the deseg-
> regation case "does not and cannot embrace all the problems
> of racial prejudice, even when problems contribute to dispro-
> portionate racial concentrations in some schools." *Swann*
> requires the removal of "state imposed" segregation. . . . The
> burden is upon the school board in this case to satisfy the
> Court that the racial composition of the schools "is not the
> result of present or past discriminatory action on their part."

His brief was a detailed defense of the board's position in the areas of (1) racial identifiability of schools, (2) racial identifiability of neigh-borhoods, and (3) busing. He recalled testimony and data that supported the claim that the faculties were mixed within one or two members of the "perfect mathematical ratio" and that schools could only be identified as white or black by their student body. He further claimed that this was caused by the racial makeup of the neighborhoods, which was not of the board's making or control.

Fowler's defense against busing was much more elaborate. He began his defense by saying:

> If the Court should find that the Board must further deseg-
> regate its schools . . . all agree that the only way to do it is by
> transporting the students to schools in buses. If the Court
> believes that this is constitutionally required, the Court should
> ask the Board to prepare a new plan. The Court should set the
> guidelines the Board must follow. Meaningful guidelines
> should consider a number of factors:
>
> 1. Which schools should the plan involve?
> 2. Mathematical ratios.

3. Maximum distance and time on buses.

4. Financing of transportation.

5. Time to develop a plan.

6. Implementation should be flexible . . .

Fowler ended his brief with the following:

> In summary, the Board of Education has continuously agreed with the *Brown* decision that no child should be excluded from any school because of the color of his skin. *Brown* did not deal with busing. The roots of the busing problem are found in *Green* in which the Court found that there was no residential segregation, and racial identification of the school system was complete and extended to every facet of school operations. The cases which govern the law in this area all come from situations where the boards have refused to recognize their obligations and the courts were shocked with the disparity between the obligations imposed by *Brown* and the facts of the case. To order a child into a distant school against the wishes of his parents and school teachers in order to remedy racial imbalance is not very different from ordering the whole family to live in the distant neighborhood to eliminate the imbalance. This solution would be unthinkable in American society. A court of equity has the power to fashion a suitable remedy without infringing upon the rights which the Court seeks to protect.[11]

Judge Taylor issued a forty-nine page memorandum opinion on March 8, 1972, stating that the Knoxville Board of Education was operating a unitary school system "consistent with constitutional requirements." The memorandum went into great detail regarding: (1) judicial history; (2) pupil locator system; (3) topography; (4) demography; (5) changes in school enrollment patterns; (6) latest changes, effective September 1972; (7) the Trotter Plan; (8) the Stolee Plan; (9)

faculty and principal assignments; (10) transfer policy; (11) extra curricular activities; (12) the building program; (13) busing; (14) *Swann* distinguished; and (15) conclusions of law.

Judge Taylor ended the order with:

> As indicated by these quotations, the standard to be achieved by school authorities is the destruction of a system which treats children differently solely on the basis of race.

> No child is excluded from any school in the Knoxville school system because of his race or color. Thus, the Knoxville system is a unitary system within the meaning of *Alexander*. As Knoxville school children are assigned to schools on the basis of their residence and without regard for their race, the system is not a dual system as defined in *Green*. Disproportionate racial mixtures in some of the Knoxville schools are the result of residential patterns. *Swann* is clear that the school authorities are not expected to prevent different treatment of the races outside the schools. 402 U.S., at 22-23. The racial composition of the Knoxville schools is not the result of present or past discriminatory action upon the part of the School Board. Knoxville is in compliance with *Swann*. Accordingly, Knoxville is operating a unitary school system consistent with constitutional requirements.

The *Knoxville Journal* headlined an editorial as "Wisdom on the Bench." The editorial ended with:

> Judge Taylor wants no accolade, to be sure. But we feel the public should realize that here is a judge who has exercised judicial sagacity intent on reaching a decision dictated to him by a combination of legal understanding, practical common sense and concern for the general public welfare; a judge who

has not allowed his intellectual honesty to be swayed by pressures of civil rights extremists. Courage as well as wisdom was on the bench.[12]

The plaintiffs followed this decision with a motion on April 4, 1972, for counsel fees and request for an additional thirty days within which to file an affidavit and brief in support of the motion. Judge Taylor granted the motion, but on April 6, 1972, issued an order and memorandum opinion that the defendants are operating a unitary school system and the plaintiffs' Motion for Immediate Relief and their subsequent applications for other relief against both the original and newly added defendant, City of Knoxville Officials, be denied, except for plaintiffs' application for attorney fees and costs, which is reserved. The case was ordered "off the docket."

On April 26, 1972, plaintiffs filed an appeal of the April 6 order. On May 1, plaintiffs' attorneys filed a memorandum in support of the motion for attorneys' fees. On the same day Judge Taylor issued an order denying the motion for attorney fees.

One week later, May 8, 1972, plaintiffs filed a motion for a new trial and/or to alter or amend the order entered May 1. On May 22, Judge Taylor issued an order denying plaintiffs' motion for a new trial and/or to alter or amend the order entered May 1. Plaintiffs filed a Notice of Appeal on May 30, and were given ninety days after the date of Notice of Appeal in which to file and docket the record in the US Sixth Circuit Court of Appeals. Filings with the appeals court were completed by the end of the month of July 1972.

The plaintiffs' appeal was heard by a panel of the Sixth Circuit Court of Appeals on February 12, 1973. The court affirmed the decision of the district court with a per curium opinion filed on March 29. Plaintiffs petitioned for a rehearing. The rehearing was granted and the rehearing in banc was held, without further oral arguments, on June 6, 1973. The previous decision was vacated. However, the court affirmed the district court's decision but remanded the case for consideration of the appellant's request for attorney's fees from the beginning of the case.

The plaintiffs had claimed that the board had not met the *Swann* requirements because there were still some one-race schools. The court ruled otherwise and supported its ruling by saying:

> While it is true that some schools in the Knoxville system will remain identifiably black or white on the basis of pupil enrollment, this is largely the result of several concentrations of blacks in the area of East Knoxville. In *Swann* the Supreme Court recognized that there are frequently concentrations of minority groups in one or more parts of a metropolitan area and the existence of a small number of racially identifiable schools in these areas is not, in and of itself, a sign that a dual system exists.

> The school authorities of Knoxville have taken affirmative actions to improve the racial mix of the schools, as required by our previous decision. Furthermore, the appellee presented evidence concerning the location of highways and railroad yards in relation to prominent topographical features, matters other than "accident or circumstance of neighborhood," from which the court was justified in finding that no plan involving the transportation of pupils between non-contiguous zones in order to further improve the racial mix within the system would be feasible at this time.

> Having found that a unitary school system exists, the District Court acted within its discretion in refusing to adopt the plaintiffs' plan which would require the busing of a large number of pupils in order to obtain a certain percentage of black students to each school in the system. As the Supreme Court said in *Swann*, 402 U.S. at page 24, 91 S. Ct. at page 1280, "The constitutional command to desegregate schools does not mean that every school in every community must always reflect the racial composition of the school system as a whole."[13]

On August 16, 1973, the Sixth Circuit Court of Appeals issued a mandate affirming the judgment of the district court. Plaintiffs appealed to the US Supreme Court for Certiorari. On February 1, 1974, the US Supreme Court denied Certiorari. *Josephine Goss v. Knoxville Board of Education* ended with little fanfare.

The remaining life of the Knoxville city schools would be troubled with complying with the Office of Civil Rights regulations pertaining to other areas of school operations, shortage of money to operate, and the politics of abandoning the system to Knox County. However, on February 1, 1974, Knoxville City School System was officially desegregated (unitary)—relatively peacefully and with minimal damage to the educational offerings.

Just how successful the process was and whether it harmed or helped the school system will be judged by time. The Knoxville school system no longer exists; the major players in the lawsuit—the judge, all four primary lawyers, the superintendents, and many of the staff and faculty members—are no longer living. The few principals and teachers still living that had a role in the desegregation process have different ideas of what really happened over the years and whether it made a difference. The process did change some of the racial attitudes, kept some of the communities intact, destroyed others, moved too slow for some, too fast for some, and was done in such a way that a majority of Knoxville citizenry does not remember much about the process at all.

Dr. Fred Bedelle Jr. and Josephine Goss Sims. This photo was taken in Detroit, Michigan, on April 30, 2012, during an interview regarding her memories of the school desegregation case. Photo courtesy of Fred Bedelle Jr.

Dr. Patricia E. Brake, in her book titled *Justice in the Valley*, said it best: "The struggle for Civil Rights in the federal courts of East Tennessee was at best long, drawn-out and difficult. Nor were the legal decisions easily enforced."[14]

The *Goss* case was an example of how a very complicated issue in conflict should be administered. Judge Taylor was true to his oath of office and was at the apex of his career. The lawyers were at times brilliant, always dedicated to representing their clients, and at times represented what society should be like. Judge Taylor was a huge baseball fan and has been quoted as saying: "The lawyers were like watching a good baseball infield in action." Judge Taylor was held in high regard by the attorneys on both sides and he respected the attorneys. The higher courts were always presented with well-prepared briefs and court documents. The citizens of greater Knoxville are fortunate to have had these five men, significant community members, and school personnel dedicated to peacefully desegregating the school system as the *Brown* decisions and subsequent court decisions required.

Judge Taylor prophetically stated in an early decision:

> Some individuals, parties to this case, will not themselves benefit from the transition. At a turning point in history some, by accidents of fate, move on to the new order. Others, by the same fate, may not. If the transition is made successfully, these plaintiffs will have had a part. Moses saw the land of Judah from Mount Pisgah, though he himself was never to set foot there.[15]

APPENDICES

APPENDIX A

JOSEPHINE GOSS and
THOMAS A. GOSS, infants
by Ralph Goss, their father
and next friend,

THOMAS L. MOORE, JR., an infant
by Thomas L. (Tommy) Moore, Sr.,
his father and next friend,

THEOTIS ROBINSON, JR., an infant
by Theotis Robinson, Sr.,
his father and next friend,

DIANNE WARD, an infant
by Berneeze A. Ward,
her father and next friend,

DONNA GRAVES, an infant
by Donald E. Graves,
her father and next friend,

PHYLLIS ROBERTS, an infant
by John B. Roberts, her father
and next friend,

ALBERT J. WINTON, JR., an infant
by Albert J. Winton, Sr., and
Mrs. Lillian Winton, his father
and mother and next friends,

REGENA ARNETT and
MICHAEL ARNETT, infants
by Mrs. Carolyn Arnett,
their mother and next friend,

ELIZABETH PEARL BARBER, an infant
by Mrs. J. E. Barber,
her mother and next friend,

SHARON SMITH, an infant
by Archibald Smith,
her father and next friend,

ANNIE BROWN, an infant
by Archibald Smith,
her guardian and next friend,

CHARLES EDMOND McAFEE, an infant
by Rev. Edmond McAfee, his father
and next friend,

CIVIL ACTION

NO. _3984_

IVAN MAURICE BLAKE, an infant,
by Rev. C. E. Blake, his father and next friend,

HERBERT THOMPSON, an infant,
by Clyde Thompson, his father and next friend,

EDDIE RIDDLE, an infant,
by Mrs. Carrie Riddle, his mother and next friend,

   and

RALPH GOSS,
THOMAS L. (TOMMY) MORE, SR.,
THEOTIS ROBINSON, SR.,
BERNEEZE A. WARD,
DONALD E. GRAVES,
JOHN B. ROBERTS,
ALBERT J. WINTON, SR.,
MRS. LILLIAN WINTON,
MRS. CAROLYN ARNETT,
MRS. J. E. BARBER,
ARCHIBALD SMITH,
REV. EDMOND McAFEE
REV. C. E. BLAKE,
CLYDE THOMPSON,
MRS. CARRIE RIDDLE

          Plaintiffs

           versus

THE BOARD OF EDUCATION OF THE CITY OF
KNOXVILLE, TENNESSEE, a body corporate
or continuous legal entity,
c/o Dr. John H. Burkhart, President;

DR. JOHN H. BURKHART, ROBERT B. RAY,
EDWARD C. WOODS, CHARLES R. MOFFETT, and
MRS. GILMER H. KEITH, as individual board
members, who acting together as such board
members constitute the Board of Education
of the City of Knoxville, Tennessee, a body
corporate or continuous legal entity;

THOMAS N. JOHNSTON, Superintendent of Schools,
of the City of Knoxville, Tennessee;

R. FRANK MARABLE, Supervisor of Child Personnel
Department, City Schools of Knoxville, Tennessee;

BUFORD A. BIBLE, Assistant and Acting Principal
of East High School, Knoxville, Tennessee;

L. GALE GARDNER, Principal of East High School,
Knoxville, Tennessee;

ROBERT H. CARDWELL, Principal of Park Junior
High School, Knoxville, Tennessee;

DONALD E. BLACKSTOCK, Principal of Mountain
View Elementary School, Knoxville, Tennessee;

WILLIAM M. DAVIS, Principal of Fulton High
School, Knoxville, Tennessee

          Defendants

COMPLAINT

1. (a) The Jurisdiction of this Court is invoked under Title 28, United States Code, section 1331. This action arises under the Fourteenth Amendment of the Constitution of the United States, section 1, and the Act of May 31, 1870, Chapter 14, section 16, 16 Stat. 144, (Title 42, United States Code, section 1981), as hereinafter more fully appears.

The matter in controversy exceeds, exclusive of interest and costs, the sum or value of Ten Thousand ($10,000.00) Dollars.

(b) The Jurisdiction of this Court is also invoked under Title 28, United States Code, section 1343. This action is authorized by the Act of April 20, 1871, Chapter 22, section 1, 17 Stat. 13, (Title 42, United States Code, section 1983), to be commenced by any citizen of the United States or other person within the jurisdiction thereof to redress the deprivation, under color of a state law, statute, ordinance, regulation, custom or usage, of rights, privileges and immunities secured by the Fourteenth Amendment of the Constitution of the United States, sec. 1, and by the Act of May 31, 1870, Chapter 14, section 16, 16 Stat. 144, (Title 42, United States Code, section 1981), providing for the equal rights of citizens and of all persons within the jurisdiction of the United States, as hereinafter more fully appears.

2. This action is a proceeding under Title 28, United States Code, sections 2201 and 2202, for a judgment declaring the rights and other legal relations of plaintiffs and other persons, similarly situated, eligible to attend elementary and secondary schools owned, maintained and operated by the City of Knoxville, Knox County, Tennessee and demanding an injunction, for the purpose of determining and redressing questions ~~matters~~ and of actual controversy between the parties, to wit:

(a) Whether the custom, policy, practice, or usage of defendants in excluding plaintiffs and other persons, similarly situated, from elementary and secondary schools owned, maintained and operated by the City of Knoxville, Knox County, Tennessee, solely because of their race or color, pursuant to Sections 49-3701, 49-3702 and 49-3703, Tennessee Code, 1955, and that portion of Section 12 of Article 11 of the Tennessee Constitution which makes it unlawful for white and colored persons to attend the same school, and pursuant to any other law, custom, policy, practice or usage violates the Fourteenth Amendment to the Constitution of the United States.

3. Plaintiffs bring this action pursuant to Rule 23 (a) (3) of the Federal Rules of Civil Procedure for themselves and on behalf of all persons similarly situated, who are so numerous as to make it impracticable to bring them all before the Court and who seek a common relief based upon common questions of law and fact.

4. Plaintiffs are Negroes and are citizens of the United States, State of Tennessee, and are residents of and domiciled in the City of Knoxville, Knox County, Eastern Division of the State of Tennessee. All of the infant plaintiffs satisfy all requirements for admission to the public elementary and secondary schools maintained and operated by the defendant Board of Education of the City of Knoxville, Tennessee in and for said City of Knoxville, Knox County, Tennessee. Adult plaintiffs, not applicants, are either parents or guardians of the infant plaintiffs who are applicants.

5. (a) The defendant, Board of Education of the City of Knoxville, Tennessee, is composed of the following board members, the defendants, Dr. John H. Burkhart, Robert B. Ray, Edward C. Woods, Charles R. Moffett and Mrs. Gilmer H. Keith, who acting together as such board members constitute the Board of Education of the City of Knoxville, Tennessee and who as such are hereinafter referred to as defendant Board of Education.

(b) Said defendant Board of Education exists pursuant to the Constitution and laws of the State of Tennessee as an administrative department or agency of the State of Tennessee, discharging governmental functions, and is by law a body corporate or a continuous body or entity, and is being sued herein as such corporate or continuous body or entity.

(c) All of said defendants, above named as board members of defendant Board of Education, are citizens and residents of the State of Tennessee, and are being sued herein in their official capacities as such board members, and are also being sued herein as individuals.

(d) Defendant Thomas N. Johnston is Superintendent of Schools of the City of Knoxville, Knox County, Tennessee and holds office pursuant to the Constitution and laws of the State of Tennessee as an administrative officer of the free public school system of Tennessee.

(e) Defendant L. Gale Gardner is principal of East High School; defendant Buford A. Bible is Assistant and Acting East High School; defendant William M. Davis is principal of
Principal of
Fulton High School; defendant Robert H. Cardwell is principal of Park Junior High School; and defendant Donald E. Blackstock is or was principal of Mountain View Elementary School; all of said schools, being public schools maintained and operated by defendant Board of Education in and for the City of Knoxville, Knox County, Tennessee.

(f) Defendant R. Frank Marable is Supervisor of the Child Personnel Department of the Knoxville City Schools and as such is an officer of the Knoxville Public School System and or agent of the defendant Board of Education and is charged with the duty of the supervision of child personnel matters in said School System, including the reception and disposition of applications by school children and or their parents for transfers of said children between schools in said School System.

(g) Defendants Thomas N. Johnston, R. Frank Marable, Buford A. Bible, L. Gale Gardner, Robert H. Cardwell, Donald E. Blackstock, and William M. Davis are citizens and residents of the State of Tennessee, and are made defendants herein and sued, in their official capacities as stated hereinabove, and are also being sued herein as individuals.

6. The State of Tennessee has declared public education a State function. The Constitution of Tennessee, Article 11, Section 12, provides:

> "Knowledge, learning and virtue, being essential to the preservation of republican institution, and the difussion of the opportunities and advantages of education throughout the different portions of the State, being highly conducive to the promotion of this end, it shall be the duty of the General Assembly, in all future periods of this Government to cherish literature and science."

Pursuant to this mandate the Legislature of Tennessee has established a uniform system of free public education in the State of Tennessee according to a plan set out in the Tennessee Code, 1955, Sections 49-101 through 49-3806, and supplements and amendments thereto. The establishment, maintenance and administration of the public school system of Tennessee is vested in a Commissioner of Education, a State Board of Education, County and City Superintendents of Public Schools, and County and City Boards of Education.

7. The public schools of the City of Knoxville, Knox County, Tennessee are under the control and supervision of defendant Board of Education and defendant Thomas N. Johnston, acting as an administrative department, **division**, or agency, and as an agent of the State of Tennessee. Said Board of Education has full power and control of all matters pertaining to the conduct of public schools within said City, and is vested with authority to exercise such other powers and perform such other duties with respect thereto as may be imposed upon them by law or ordinance by

virture of the legislative acts of the State of Tennessee. Said
Board of Education is under a duty to enforce the school laws of
the State of Tennessee; to maintain an efficient system of public
schools in the City of Knoxville, Knox County, Tennessee; to determine the studies to be pursued, the methods of teaching, and to
establish such schools as may be necessary to the completeness
and efficiency of the school system. Defendant, Thomas N.
Johnston, as Superintendent, has the immediate control of the
operation of public schools of said City and is the administrative
agent of the defendant Board of Education.

        8. (a) Defendant Board of Education maintains and
operates in and for the said City of Knoxville a number of public
elementary and secondary schools, including those designated as
Mountain View Elementary, Park Junior High, East High and Fulton
High Schools, exclusively for the education, convenience and use
of white school children residing in the City of Knoxville. All
of these schools afford adequate facilities to provide elementary
and secondary instruction on a modern basis by grades. These
schools, except Fulton High School, are readily accessible to, and
are used by white school children residing in the areas proximately surrounding the respective schools; but the facilities offered by these schools are denied by defendants to the infant
plaintiffs and other Negro children, similarly situated, who reside in the areas proximately surrounding said schools, solely
because of their race or color.

        (b) Fulton High School affords adequate facilities
to provide technical and vocational instruction on a modern basis
by grades. Fulton High School is used by white children residing
in the City of Knoxville, Tennessee who desire said technical and

vocational instruction irrespective of their place of residence
in the City; but the facilities afforded by Fulton High School are
denied by defendants to infant plaintiffs who desire said instruction, and other Negro children, similarly situated, residing

in the City of Knoxville, Tennessee irrespective of their place
of residence in the City, solely on account of their race or
color.

       9. (a) At the beginning of the Fall Term or Semester,
September 2, 1959, infant plaintiffs, Thomas L. Moore, Jr.,
Albert Winton, Jr. and Dianne Ward, presented themselves and made
proper and timely application for admission to Mountain View
Elementary School; infant plaintiffs, Josephine Goss, Phyllis
Roberts, Elizabeth Pearl Barber, Theotis Robinson, Jr., Sharon
Smith, Annie Brown and Ivan Maurice Blake, presented themselves
and made proper and timely application for admission to East
High School, and infant plaintiffs, Herbert Thompson and Eddie
Riddle, presented themselves and made proper and timely application to Fulton High School; but all of said plaintiffs were
refused admission by defendant Donald E. Blackstock, Principal
of Mountain View Elementary School; defendant Buford A. Bible,
Acting and Assistant Principal of East High School; and defendant
William M. Davis, Principal of Fulton High School, respectively,
to said respective schools, solely on account of plaintiffs'
race or color. On the same day September 2, 1959, all of these
applicants presented themselves to the defendant R. Frank Marable,
Supervisor of the Child Personnel Department, and the defendant
Thomas N. Johnston, Superintendent of City Schools, and appealed
from the action of the defendant Donald E. Blackstock, Principal
of Mountain View Elementary School; the defendant Buford A. Bible,
Assistant and Acting Principal of East High School and the defendant William M. Davis, Principal of Fulton High School, respectively, in denying and refusing the admission of said infant
children to said schools solely because of their race or color;
and thereupon, said infant plaintiffs, Thomas L. Moore, Jr.,
Albert Winton, Jr. and Dianne Ward, made application to said defendants, R. Frank Marable, Supervisor of Child Personnel Department and Thomas N. Johnston, Superintendent of City Schools for

transfer from Eastport Elementary School, a school designated by defendants exclusively for Negroes, to said Mountain View School; and said infant plaintiffs, Josephine Goss, Phyllis Roberts, Elizabeth Pearl Barber, Theotis Robinson, Jr., Sharon Smith, Annie Brown and Ivan Maurice Blake, made application to said defendant officials for transfer from Austin High School, a school designated by defendants exclusively for Negroes, to said East High School on the ground that said Mountain View Elementary School and said East High School, respectively, were nearer their place of residence than the Eastport Elementary School and Austin High School, respectively. The aforesaid infant plaintiffs reside in the areas served by said respective schools to which they made application, and if they were white children, they would have been transferred and admitted to said schools but all ten of said plaintiffs were refused admission by said defendants to said respective schools, solely on account of their race or color. Defendants require Negro applicants to attend schools designated exclusively for Negro children, without regard to the proximity of the school.

(b) The said infant plaintiffs, Herbert Thompson and Eddie Riddle, made application to said defendant officials, R. Frank Marable, Supervisor of the Child Personnel Department and Thomas N. Johnston, Superintendent of City Schools, for transfer from Austin High School, a school designated by defendants exclusively for Negroes, to Fulton High School on the ground that they desired to take certain technical and vocational courses at Fulton High School which school afforded adequate facilities for said technical and vocational instruction on a modern basis to the pupils of the City of Knoxville irrespective of their place of residence, and if they were white children they would have been transferred and admitted to said school, but said two infant plaintiffs were refused admission by said defendant officials to said Fulton High School, solely on account of their race or color.

(c) On the following day, September 3, 1959, the infant plaintiff, Donna Graves, presented herself and made proper and timely application for admission to said East High School on

16.

the ground that said East High School was nearer her place of residence than the Austin High School. Said Plaintiff resides in the area served by East High School to which she made application and if she were a white child she would have been admitted to said school, but said Plaintiff was refused admission to said East High School by said defendant Buford A. Bible, Assistant and Acting Principal of East High School, solely on account of her race or color. On the same day, September 3, 1959, the said applicant, Donna Graves, presented herself to the defendant, R. Frank Marable, Supervisor of the Child Personnel Department and appealed from the action of the said defendant Buford A. Bible, Assistant and Acting Principal of East High School in denying and refusing the admission of said child to said school solely because of her race or color; and thereupon, she made application for transfer from said Austin High School to said East High School on the ground that said East High School is nearer her place of residence than said Austin High School. Said infant plaintiff resides in an area served by said East High School to which she made application and if she were a white child she would have been transferred and admitted to East High School but said plaintiff was refused admission by said defendant R. Frank Marable to said East High School solely on account of race or color. Said plaintiff made several attempts to see said defendant Thomas N. Johnston, Superintendent of City Schools, but without success.

(d) The plaintiff, Ralph Goss, who is father and next friend of the infant plaintiff, Thomas A. Goss, presented himself on said September 2, 1959 to said defendant R. Frank Marable, Supervisor of the Child Personnel Department and then to defendant Thomas N. Johnston, Superintendent of City Schools on behalf of his said son, who was not present, for admission to Park Junior High School; and thereupon requested a transfer for his said son and infant plaintiff from Vine Junior High School, a school designated by defendants exclusively for Negroes, to said Park Junior High School on the ground that said Park Junior High School is nearer his place of residence than the said Vine Junior High School. Said infant plaintiff is required by defendants to attend said Vine Junior High School notwithstanding said Park Junior High School is nearer his place of residence than said Vine Junior High School. Said infant plaintiff resides in an area served by said Park Junior High School to which he made application as aforesaid and if he were a white child, he would have been admitted as aforesaid but said infant plaintiff, through his father and next friend, was refused admission by said defendants to said Park Junior High School, solely on account of said plaintiff's race or color.

(e) The infant plaintiffs, Regena Arnett, Michael Arnett and Charles Edmond McAfee, through their respective plaintiff parents and next friends, Mrs. Carolyn Arnett and Reverend Edmond McAfee, are applicants for admission to said Mountain View Elementary School. Although neither said infant plaintiffs nor their said plaintiff parents and next friends presented themselves to said defendant officials, the said adult plaintiffs did, with other parents, petition the defendant Board and Superintendent to desegregate the public schools of the City of Knoxville, Tennessee this year, beginning the fall term of 1959. Said infant plaintiffs are required to attend said Eastport Elementary School, a school designated by defendants exclusively for Negroes, notwithstanding the Mountain View Elementary School is nearer their place of residence than the said Eastport Elementary School. Said infant plaintiffs reside in the area served by said Mountain View Elementary School and would have been admitted there if they were white children. The infant plaintiffs Michael Arnett and Charles Edmond McAfee are attending school for the first time in their

-9-

lives, being now enrolled in the first grade. These aforesaid infant plaintiffs are being refused admission to said Mountain View Elementary School solely on account of their race or color on the basis of the aforesaid petition by said Plaintiff and other parents to desegregate the Public Schools of Knoxville being denied by defendant Board and on the basis of the Board's formal action not to desegregate the Public Schools of Knoxville this school year, as more fully hereinafter set forth.

      (f) On November 4, 1959 the said Mountain View School was closed by defendant Board of Education and the white children attending school there were transferred to another school also designated by defendants for the exclusive use of white school children. Plaintiffs are informed and believe, and therefore aver upon information and belief, that defendants closed the said Mountain View School for the purpose and with the intention of reopening and designating the same at a subsequent date as a segregated school for the exclusive use of Negro school children.

      (g) A committee of five of the adult plaintiffs, to-wit: Ralph Goss, B. A. Ward, Tommy Moore, Theotis Robinson, Sr. and Clyde Thompson, representing all of the infant and adult plaintiffs, and on behalf of other Negro parents and children of school age and similarly situated, filed a formal Request and Appeal in writing with defendant Board of Education at its regular meeting on September 14, 1959 and which, inter alia, was an appeal to the defendant Board of Education from the action of the aforesaid defendant principals, defendant Supervisor of Child Personnel Department and the defendant Superintendent of City Schools in denying and refusing the admission and transfer of said infant plaintiffs to the aforesaid elementary and secondary schools of the City of Knoxville, Tennessee, solely on account of their race or color, and they further requested that said

Negro children be enrolled now in the schools to which they applied as aforesaid.

The said appeal and request was denied by the defendant
Board of Education--it took no action thereon and it has continued
to maintain and enforce its previous decision to continue pursuing and enforcing its policy of compulsory racial segregation in
the public schools of Knoxville.

10. The defendants rely on the following provisions of
the Tennessee Constitution and Statutes, which read as follows:

Constitution of 1870, Art. 11, Sec. 12:

"....No school established or aided under this
section shall allow white and negro children to
be received as scholars together in the same
school...."

Tennessee Code, 1955, Sections:

"49-3701. Interracial Schools prohibited.- It
shall be unlawful for any school, academy,
college, or other place of learning to allow
white and colored persons to attend the same
school, academy, college, or other place of
learning. (Acts 1901, ch. 7, sec 1; Shan.,
sec 6888a37; Code 1932, sec 11395.)

"49-3702. Teaching of mixed classes prohibited.-
It shall be unlawful for any teacher, professor,
or educator in any college, academy, or school
of learning, to allow the white and colored races
to attend the same school, or for any teacher or
educator, or other person to instruct or teach
both the white and colored races in the same class,
school, or college building, or in any other place
or places of learning, or allow or permit the same
to be done with their knowledge, consent or pro-
curement. (Acts 1901, ch. 7, sec 2; Shan., sec
6888a38; Code 1932, sec 11396.)

"49-3703. Penalty for violations.- Any person
violating any of the provisions of this chapter,
shall be guilty of a misdemeanor, and, upon
conviction, shall be fined for each offense
fifty dollars ($50.00), and imprisonment not less
than thirty (30) days nor more than six (6)
months. (Acts 1901, ch. 7, sec 3;
Shan., sec 6888a39; mod. Code 1932, sec 11397.)

11. The defendant Board of Education has maintained
and operated, and continues to maintain and operate racially

-11-

segregated elementary and secondary schools for the use of white
and Negro children and to enforce a policy and practice of compulsory racial segregation in the City Schools of Knoxville as
averred herein above. On a number of occasions, beginning with
the year of 1954, petitions were presented to the defendant Board
of Education by Negro parents of school age children residing in
Knoxville, Tennessee, requesting defendants to eliminate the unconstitutional racial segregation here complained of in the public
City schools of said City. Said defendant has failed and refused
to grant said petitions.

On July 12, 1954 at a regular meeting of defendant
Board, a number of parents of Negro children of school age and
citizens of the City of Knoxville, Tennessee personally appeared
before the defendant Board in support of a petition which previously had been filed with said defendant Board to take immediate
action towards desegregating the public schools of the City of
Knoxville in accordance with the holding of the Supreme Court of
the United States that racial segregation in public education is
unconstitutional and void as being in violation of the equal protection clause of the Fourteenth Amendment to the Constitution of
the United States; and they also requested a meeting with the
Board to discuss the matter, but said petition and request were
refused. Seventeen Negro parents of children of school age on or
about July 8, 1955 and Forty Negro parents of children of school
age on Aug. 13, 1955 on behalf of themselves and on behalf of other
Negro parents school children similarly situated petitioned the
Board of Education of the City of Knoxville to abolish racial
segregation in the public schools of Knoxville and to work out a
plan for desegregation in the public schools but not later than
September 1955 and that desegregation be completed by not later
than the school term beginning September 1956. Said defendant
failed and refused to grant said petitions.

-12-

On August 17, 1955, the defendant Board issued a formal Statement of Policy declaring that it would act in good faith and would proceed to make a reasonable start in desegregating the public schools and that it had instructed the defendant Superintendent and his Staff to develop a specific plan of action leading to gradual integration of Knoxville Public Schools, but on May 14, 1956 at a regular Board meeting it was announced that the Board had decided to delay indefinitely the formulation and inauguration of a plan of desegregation of our public schools.

On June 7, 1956 the defendant Board was petitioned by the said Negro parents to rescind its said decision to delay indefinitely desegregation of the public schools but said petition was ignored by defendant Board.

Again, on June 11, 1956 at a regular Board meeting a large number of Negro parents of children of school age and other citizens personally appeared before the defendant Board of Education and petitioned said Board to reconsider its immediate previous action or decision, and proceed to desegregate the public schools, but the said Board upon motion duly made and seconded voted unanimously that "we answer their petition with the word 'No'".

The Board further emphasized its decision not to ~~disc~~ ~~~~~~~~~~~ desegregate the public schools and its continued policy and practice of compulsory racial segregation; when at the beginning of the school term on September 4, 1956 it denied Negro pupils admission to certain schools solely on account of race or color, and subsequently resisted an action filed on January 7, 1957 in the District Court of the United States For The Eastern District of Tennessee, Northern Division, by said children and their parents seeking declaratory relief and admission to the public schools of Knoxville on a racially unsegregated basis and without discrimination on account of race or

color. On June 1, 1959 said action was dismissed against three
of the members of the defendant Board on a procedural question.

Twenty Negro parents of children of school age, nine of
whom are adult plaintiffs, on or about July 9, 1959 petitioned
the defendant Board to consider on or prior to its regular meeting
on July 13, 1959 the admission of their children this fall (1959)
to the public schools of the City of Knoxville, Tennessee, for
which said children are qualified, on a racially unsegregated
basis and without discrimination on account of race or color.
They further requested **said** Board to eliminate racial segregation
in the public schools of Knoxville, that the Board work out a
plan for desegregation as soon as possible, and that concrete
steps towards desegregation be put into effect the next school
term. Other citizens of Knoxville personally appeared with said
petitioners before the Board at its said regular meeting and
joined in the aforesaid request of Petitioners. The defendant
Board failed and refused to take any action on said petition.

Again, at the regular meeting of the defendant Board on
August 10, 1959, Negro parents of children of school age and
other citizens requested a decision as to desegregating the public
schools the next school term (Fall of 1959). The members of the
Board decided to discuss the matter in Executive session, which
they did at that time. Shortly thereafter, it was announced by
defendant Board in open meeting on said August 10, 1959 that the
formal motion voted by the Board states that it "publicly an-
nounces that it does not intend to integrate the schools at this
time but will continue to study the problem".

Again, on September 14, 1959, being after the infant
plaintiffs were refused admission to certain schools because of
their race or color as more particularly averred hereinabove, a
group of parents of children of school age and other citizens

personally appeared before the Board and with the aforesaid
Plaintiffs joined in an appeal to the defendant Board to admit
the Negro children now to the schools for which they recently applied and were refused by said defendants on account of race or
color; and they further requested the Board to rescind its decision not to desegregate the schools this year; and they further
requested the Board to desegregate the schools and adopt a plan
for desegregation and elimination of racial discrimination this
school year. Defendant Board refused to grant the Appeal and
Request, or to take any action thereon.

The defendant, Board of Education, has had two meetings
since the said September 14, 1959 meeting, to-wit a called meeting
on October 5, 1959 and a regular meeting on November 9, 1959. No
report has been made of the defendant Board of Education taking
any action to admit said plaintiffs to the respective schools for
which they applied or to eliminate racial segregation in the
public schools of Knoxville. The said defendant Board has maintained and operated, and continues to maintain and operate
racially segregated public elementary and secondary schools for
the use of white and Negro children in the City of Knoxville, and
to enforce its declared policy and practice of compulsory racial
segregation in the public schools of said City.

12. The infant plaintiffs and all other persons, similarly situated, in the City of Knoxville, Knox County, Tennessee,
are thereby deprived of their rights guaranteed by the Constitution and laws of the United States.

Plaintiffs aver that the said constitutional and statutory provisions and all other laws, customs, policies, practices
andusages of the State of Tennessee requiring or permitting segregation of the races in public education fall within the prohibited group which the Supreme Court of the United States holds

must yield to the Fourteenth Amendment of the Constitution of the United States; and in addition, the Supreme Court of Tennessee has held that said segregation laws of the State of Tennessee violate the Fourteenth Amendment of the Constitution of the United States, and are of no force and effect.

Plaintiffs therefore aver that the said custom, policy, practice or usage of defendants in excluding plaintiffs and other persons, similarly situated, from elementary and secondary schools, owned, maintained and operated by the City of Knoxville, solely because of their race or color, pursuant to said constitutional and statutory provisions and any other law, custom, policy, practice or usage of the State of Tennessee requiring or permitting segregation of the Negro and white races in public education, violates the Fourteenth Amendment to the Constitution of the United States, and is therefore unconstitutional and void and affords defendants no legal excuse to deprive plaintiffs of their rights herein prayed.

13. Plaintiffs and those similarly situated and affected, on whose behalf this suit is brought, are suffering irreparable injury and are threatened with irreparable injury in the future by reason of the acts herein complained of. They have no plain, adequate or complete remedy to redress the wrongs and illegal acts herein complained of other than this suit for a declaration of rights and an injunction. Any other remedy to which plaintiffs and those similarly situated could be remitted would be attended by such uncertainties and delays as to deny substantial relief, would involve multiplicity of suits, cause further irreparable injury and occasion damage, vexation and inconvenience, not only to the plaintiffs and those similarly situated, but to defendants as governmental agencies.

Plaintiffs further aver that for over five (5) years the defendants and/or their predecessors have had notice that the

-16-

policy and practice of compulsory racial segregation which they
are enforcing is unconstitutional and void. Many of the infant
plaintiffs were small children when defendants first received
that notice. These plaintiffs have been deprived of their right
to a racially unsegregated and non-discriminatory education in
the public schools for this long period of time, and each additional day or month of such deprivation brings them closer and
closer to complete exclusion from and loss of that constitutional
right, to their immediate and lasting harm and damage. In addition, at least two of the infant plaintiffs were entering the
first grade this year. These infants had not been subjected to
or indoctrinated with the racial prejudices, segregation and discrimination in public education enforced by defendants. Whether
defendants require these first graders to continue in the racially segregated school in which defendants compelled them to enroll
in September, 1959, or whether defendants re-open Mountain View
Elementary School as one segregated for exclusive attendance by
Negro children and then transfer said first grade plaintiffs to
that school, these infant plaintiffs are in either case being
subjected for the first time to the inherent evil, inequality and
humiliation of the unconstitutional compulsory racial segregation,
to their immediate and lasting harm and damage.

Plaintiffs are advised that the next school term or
semester in the City Schools of Knoxville begins on ___ January
1960, so that unless the defendants are immediately restrained
from pursuing and enforcing their unlawful action in refusing to
admit the individual named infant plaintiffs, said plaintiffs
will suffer the immediate and irreparable injuries and damages as
set out above.

14. There is between the parties an actual controversy
as hereinbefore set forth.

WHEREFORE PLAINTIFFS respectfully pray that:

The Court issue forthwith a temporary restraining order against the defendants, immediately restraining and enjoining them and each of them, their officers, attorneys, agents, employees, successors in office, and all persons in active concert and participation with them from refusing to admit or transfer the infant plaintiffs, Thomas L. Moore, Jr., Albert Winton, Jr., Dianne Ward, Regena Arnett, Michael Arnett and Charles Edmond McAfee, to the Mountain View Elementary School, the infant plaintiff, Thomas A. Goss, to the Park Junior High School, the infant plaintiffs, Josephine Goss, Phyllis Roberts, Elizabeth Pearl Barber, Theotis Robinson, Jr., Sharon Smith, Annie Brown, Ivan Maurice Blake and Donna Graves, to East High School, and the infant plaintiffs, Herbert Thompson and Eddie Riddle, to Fulton High School, or any other public school maintained and/or operated by them in and for the City of Knoxville, Knox County, Tennessee, on account of plaintiffs race or color, pending further orders of the Court.

The Court issue a preliminary injunction restraining and enjoining the defendants and each of them, their officers, attorneys, agents, employees, successors in office, and all persons in active concert and participation with them, as of the first day of the next school term or semester beginning in January, 1960, from refusing to admit or transfer the infant plaintiffs, Thomas L. Moore, Jr., Albert Winton, Jr., Dianne Ward, Regena Arnett, Michael Arnett and Charles Edmond McAfee, to the Mountain View Elementary School, the infant plaintiff, Thomas A. Goss, to the Park Junior High School, the infant plaintiffs, Josephine Goss, Phyllis Roberts, Elizabeth Pearl Barber, Theotis Robinson, Jr., Sharon Smith, Annie Brown, Ivan Maurice Blake and Donna Graves, to East High School and the infant plaintiffs, Herbert Thompson and Eddie Riddle, to Fulton High School, or any other public school maintained and/or operated by them in and for the City of Knoxville,

Knox County, Tennessee, because of their race or color, pending further orders of the Court.

The Court adjudge, decree and declare the rights and legal relations of the parties to the subject matter herein controversy in order that such declaration shall have the force and effect of a final judgment or decree.

The Court enter a judgment or decree declaring that the custom, policy, practice or usage of defendants in excluding plaintiffs and other persons, similarly situated, from Mountain View Elementary School, Park Junior High School, East High School, Fulton High School, or any other public elementary or secondary schools maintained and operated by defendant Board of Education in and for the City of Knoxville, Knox County, Tennessee, solely because of race, pursuant to the above quoted portion of Article 11, Section 12 of the Constitution of Tennessee, Secion 49-3701, 49-3702, 49-3703 of the Tennessee Code, 1955, and any other law, custom, policy, practice and usage, violates the Fourteenth Amendment of the United States Constitution, and is therefore un-constitutional and void.

The Court issue a permanent injunction forever re-straining and enjoining defendants, and each of them, their of-ficers, attorneys, agents, employees, successors in office, and all persons in active concert and participation with them, from enforcing and pursuing the policy, practice, custom, and usage of requiring or permitting racial segregation in the operation of the public schools of the City of Knoxville, and from engaging in any and all action which limits or affects admission to, atten-dance in, or education of the infant plaintiffs, or any other Negro children similarly situated, in schools under defendants' jurisdiction, on the basis of race or color.

That in addition to the immediate and preliminary re-lief prayed hereinabove in behalf of the named infant plaintiffs individually, the Court also issue expeditiously an order in behalf of the plaintiffs and all other persons similarly situated, requiring the defendants to present to this Court, a complete plan, adopted by them, which is designed to bring about good faith compliance with the decision of the Supreme Court of the United States in <u>Brown</u> v <u>Board of Education</u>, 347 U. S. 483, 74 S. Ct. 686, 98 L. Ed. 873, 38 A. L. R. (ad) 1180, 349 U. S. 294, 75 S. Ct. 753, 99 L. Ed. 1083, at the earliest practicable date throughout the Public School System of the City of Knoxville, Knox County, Tennessee; and which shall provide for a prompt and reasonable start towards desegregation of the public schools of said City and a systematic and effective method for achieving such desegregation with all deliberate speed.

 Plaintiffs further pray that the Court will allow them their costs and such further, other or additional relief as may appear to the Court to be equitable and just.

Carl A. Cowan
CARL A. COWAN
101½ W. Vine Avenue
Knoxville 2, Tennessee

Z Alexander Looby
Avon N. Williams Jr.
Z. ALEXANDER LOOBY and
AVON N. WILLIAMS, JR.
327 Charlotte Avenue
Nashville 3, Tennessee

Jack Greenberg
Thurgood Marshall
JACK GREENBERG and
THURGOOD MARSHALL
10 Columbus Circle
New York 19, New York

Attorneys For Plaintiffs

V E R I F I C A T I O N

STATE OF TENNESSEE)
) SS
COUNTY OF KNOX)

          Ralph Goss, Thomas L. Moore, Theotis Robinson, Sr.,
Berneeze A. Ward, Donald E. Graves, John B. Roberts,
Albert J. Winton, Sr., Mrs. Lillian E. Winton, Carolyn Arnett,
Mrs. J. E. Barber, Archibald Smith, Rev. Edmond McAfee,
Rev. C. E. Blake, Clyde Thompson and Mrs. Carrie Riddle
make oath that they are plaintiffs in the above case; that they
have read and know the contents of their foregoing Complaint and
that the statements made therein are true as of their own knowledge,
except as to these statements which are stated therein to be made
therein upon information and belief, and those statements they
believe to be true.

                  Signed: *Ralph Goss*
                       Thomas L. Moore
                       Theotis Robinson Sr.
                       Berneeze A. Ward
                       Donald E. Graves
                       John B. Roberts
                       Albert J. Winton Sr.
                       Mrs Lillian E. Winton
                       Carolyn Arnett
                       Mrs J. E. Barber
                       Archibald Smith
                       Rev. Edmond McAfee
                       Rev. C. E. Blake
                       Clyde Thompson
                       Mrs Carrie Riddle

        Sworn to and subscribed before me, C. A. Cowan, a Notary
Public in and for said State and County, the 9th day of December,
1959.
                     C. A. Cowan Notary Public

     My commission expires April 18, 1960.

N O T I C E

TO THE DEFENDANTS NAMED IN THE CAPTION

HEREIN ABOVE IN THIS CAUSE:

Please take Notice that the plaintiffs, named in the caption hereinabove in this cause, having filed their verified Complaint together with Motions for temporary restraining order and a preliminary injunction against the said defendants, the undersigned will appear before the Honorable Robert L. Taylor, United States District Judge, at 9 A. M. o'clock, on Friday, January 8, 1960, in the United States District Courtroom, Knoxville, Tennessee, and ask the Court to issue and Order to Show Cause why a Temporary Restraining Order and/or Preliminary Injunction should not issue on or before January 15, 1960 /against the said defendants, for the purpose of immediately restraining and enjoining them, and each of them, their officers, attorneys, agents, employees, successors in office, and all persons in active concert and participation with them, either forthwith or as of the first day of the next school term or semester beginning in January, 1960, from refusing to admit or transfer the infant plaintiffs, Thomas L. Moore, Jr., Albert Winton, Jr., Dianne Ward, Regena Arnett, Michael Arnett and Charles Edmond McAfee, to the Mountain View Elementary School, the infant plaintiff, Thomas A. Goss, to the Park Junior High School, the infant plaintiffs, Josephine Goss, Phyllis Roberts, Elizabeth Pearl Barber, Theotis Robinson, Jr., Sharon Smith, Annie Brown, Ivan Maurice Blake and Donna Graves, to East High School, and the infant plaintiffs, Herbert Thompson and Eddie Riddle, to Fulton High School, or any other public school maintained and/or operated by them in and for the City of Knoxville, Knox County, Tennessee, on account of Plaintiff's race or color, pending further orders of the Court.

This 11th day of December, 1959   *Carl A. Cowan*
                                   Attorney for Plaintiffs

-22-

APPENDIX B

T. N. JOHNSTON
SUPERINTENDENT

A. C. HUTSON, JR.
BUSINESS MANAGER

Knoxville City Schools
BOARD OF EDUCATION BLDG.
FIFTH AVE. AT CENTRAL
KNOXVILLE 17, TENNESSEE

TO THE HONORABLE ROBERT L. TAYLOR
JUDGE OF THE U. S. DISTRICT COURT AT KNOXVILLE

On Wednesday, March 30, 1960 at a meeting of the Board of Education duly held, the Superintendent of the Public Schools of Knoxville, speaking for himself and the administrative staff, recommended that the Board adopt the following plan of desegregation called "Plan No. 9":

"1. Effective with the beginning of the 1960-61 school year racial segregation in Grade One of the Knoxville Public Schools is discontinued.

2. Effective for 1961-62 school year racial segregation shall be discontinued in Grade Two and thereafter in the next higher Grade at the beginning of each successive school year until the Desegregation Plan is effected in all twelve grades.

3. Each student entering a desegregated grade in the Knoxville Public Schools will be permitted to attend the school designated for the Zone in which he or she legally resides, subject to regulations that may be necessary in particular instances.

4. A plan of school zoning or districting based upon the location and capacity (size) of school buildings and the latest enrollment studies without reference to race will be established for the administration of the first grade and other grades as hereafter desegregated.

5. Requests for transfer of students in desegregated grades from the school of their Zone to another school will be given full consideration and will be granted when made in writing by parents or guardians or those acting in the position of parents, when good cause therefor is shown and when transfer is practicable, consistent with sound school administration.

6. The following will be regarded as some of the valid conditions to support requests for transfer:

    a. When a white student would otherwise be required to attend a school previously serving colored students only;

    b. When a colored student would otherwise be required to attend a school previously serving white students only;

    c. When a student would otherwise be required to attend a school where the majority of students of that school or in his or her grade are of a different race."

TO THE HONORABLE ROBERT L. TAYLOR   Page 2

Said meeting was adjourned to convene again before April 8, 1960 and
the adjourned meeting was regularly reconvened on Monday, April 4, 1960
at 7:30 P.M. when the following resolution was moved by Dr. Charles
Moffett and seconded by Mr. Roy Linville and adopted:

> "I move that the Board follow the recommendation of the
> Superintendent and submit Plan No. 9 to the Federal Judge
> on April 8, 1960."

I hereby certify that the foregoing resolution was properly adopted by
the Board of Education of Knoxville, Tennessee at a meeting duly held
on April 4, 1960.

April 5, 1960

_____   _____
                      President   Secretary

APPENDIX C

IN THE UNITED STATES DISTRICT COURT FOR
THE EASTERN DISTRICT OF TENNESSEE,
NORTHERN DIVISION.

JOSEPHINE GOSS, ET AL.,

                    PLAINTIFFS, Ⅹ

                                 Ⅹ

          VS.   Ⅹ CIVIL CAUSE NO. 3984

                                 Ⅹ

BOARD OF EDUCATION OF THE   Ⅹ
CITY OF KNOXVILLE, TENNESSEE,
ET AL.,

                    DEFENDANTS.

STATEMENT OF PLAN OF DESEGREGATION FILED
IN CONFORMITY WITH ORDER OF JULY 30, 1965.

The Plan for Complete Desegregation of the schools
of the City of Knoxville, Tennessee, which emerges from the
various Plans, Objections, Amendments and Court Orders in this
cause is as follows:

1. Effective with the beginning of the school year in
    September, 1964, all racially discriminatory prac-
    tices in all grades, programs and facilities of the
    Knoxville Public School System shall be eliminated
    and abolished. Without limiting the generality and
    effectiveness of the foregoing, all teachers,
    principals and other school personnel shall be employed
    by defendants and assigned or re-assigned to schools
    on the basis of educational need and other academic
    considerations, and without regard to race or color
    of the persons to be assigned, and without regard
    to the race or color of the children attending the
    particular school or class within a school to which
    the person is to be assigned. No transfer or re-
    transfer of a teacher, principal or other school
    personnel may be granted or required for considera-
    tions based upon race and color and no assignment or
    re-assignment of such teacher, principal or other
    school personnel may be made for considerations based
    upon race or color.

All tenure and seniority rights are to be observed and the defendants will not utilize or attempt to utilize the provisions of the State Teacher Tenure Law or any other law, custom or regulation conferring discretion upon them in the employment and discharge of teachers or the abolition of teaching positions in such manner as to discriminate either directly or indirectly on account of race or color in the employment, discharge, re-employment, assignment, or re-assignment of teachers, principals or other school personnel in the Knoxville City School System.

2. Each student will be assigned to the school designated for the district in which he or she legally resides, subject to variations due to overcrowding and other transfers for cause, and the Superintendent may permit continued enrollment of students in their present schools until completion of the grade requirements for said school, provided this is consistent with sound school administrative policy.

3. A plan of school districting based upon the location and capacity (size) of school buildings and the latest enrollment studies will be followed subject to modifications from time to time as required. (Zone maps and typed statements of Zone boundaries were filed in this case April 27, 1965).

4. Upon written application, students may be permitted to transfer to schools outside their assigned attendance zones only in exceptional cases for objective administrative reasons and no transfers shall be granted, denied or required because of race or color. All applications of students for transfers to schools outside their assigned attendance zones shall be considered and approved by the Superintendent of Schools pursuant to recommendation of the Director of the Department of Child Personnel after due investigation and consideration of the Department of Child Personnel.

5. Students may request transfer to or enrollment in any vocational or technical facility sponsored by the Knoxville City Board of Education and will be accepted subject to requirements respecting aptitude, ability, pre-training, physical condition, age, and other considerations including adequacy of facilities.

6. The Board of Education recognizes the continuation of jurisdiction of the United States District Court for the Eastern District of Tennessee, Northern Division, at Knoxville of this Board and the matters involved in this plan, until termination of said jurisdiction by express direction of said court.

The foregoing statement of Plan is filed pursuant to the order entered by this court on July 30, 1965, directing that the

Plan be embodied in a single document. The sources of the various paragraphs set out above are as follows:

Paragraphs 1, 2(first part), 3 (first sentence), 5 and 6 were taken verbatim from the "Amended Plan for Complete Desegregation" filed pursuant to order of the court entered February 12, 1965, and which was the target for objections filed by the plaintiffs which were considered at the pre-trial hearing of July 28, 1965.

Paragraph 2, the last part beginning with the words "and the Superintendent may permit" was added by virtue of the declaration of policy of the Board of Education made on April 19, 1965.

Paragraph 4 is drawn from paragraphs 1 and 2 of the court order entered July 30, 1965. It was deemed that those two sentences, drawn from that order, displaced paragraph 4 as set out in the "Amended Plan for Complete Desegregation" filed on February 15, 1965.

_____
**Attorney for Defendant Board
of Education**

I hereby certify that three copies of the foregoing have been served by mailing upon Carl Cowan, one of the attorneys for the plaintiffs, this August   , 1965.

_____

APPENDIX D

KNOXVILLE TEACHERS LEAGUE

The Knoxville Teachers League voted on March 8 to invoke sanctions beginning April 13, 1966, because Knoxville City Council failed to appropriate the Board of Education's budget request by a little more than a million dollars.

One part of this program is a withholding of Extra-curricular, Non-compensated activities.

T H E K N O X V I L L E T E A C H E R S L E A G U E

TEACHERS' NON-COMPENSATED EXTRA CURRICULAR ACTIVITIES

Based upon the survey that each school was asked to turn in, a committee of Classroom Teachers compiled the following list of non-compensated extra curricular activities. This list has been approved by the Executive Board and will be the one used in invoking Sanction D (A program of withdrawal and/or curtailment of non-compensated extra curricular services and activities) beginning on April 13 unless some negotiation takes place between the League and City Officials by April 7.

However, it should be remembered that, according to our contracts, we are compensated for 15 minutes before the opening of school and 15 minutes after the dismissal of school. Therefore, if any of the following activities are conducted during the regular work day, for which of course we are compensated, it should be understood that these activities would not be curtailed.

1. CLUBS - Sponsoring, Supervising, and Chaperoning:

    Algebra, Anchor, Art, Beta, Bowling, Campus Book, Cheerleaders, *Future Homemakers of America, Future Physicians and Nurses, Future Teachers of America, Garden, Gray Y, Hi-Y, Ice Hockey, Key, Language, Latin, Literary, Modern Dance, National Honor Society, Pet, Quill and Scroll, Rhythm Band, Speech and Drama League, Student Council, Teens for Christ, Trade and Industry, Typing, Varsity, Y'ette, etc.

2. TRIPS - Sponsoring, Supervising, and Chaperoning:

    Carousal, Conventions, Festivals, Field trips, Hikes, Outings, Picnics, Safety Patrol trips, Tours, etc.

3. Detention sessions, Early morning duty, Hall duty, Study Halls.

4. CONVENTIONS AND REGIONAL MEETINGS:

    Future Homemakers of America*, Future Teachers of America, National Honor Society, State Debate Tourney, Student Council State Convention, etc.

5. SOCIAL ACTIVITIES - Sponsoring, Supervising, and Chaperoning:

    Athletic Banquet, Basketball Banquet, Boys' Octet, Carnival, Dances, Delta Kappa Gamma Contest, Fashion Show, Home Economics Banquet, Kite Day, Parties, Pep Meetings, Proms, 7th and 8th Grade Banquets, 6th Grade Banquet, Senior Breakfast, Talent Shows, Teas, etc.

6. MUSIC ACTIVITIES - Sponsoring, Supervising, and Chaperoning:

    All State Chorus, Carnival, Concerts, Festivals, Opera, Operetta, Orchestra Audition, Parades, Rehearsals, Special Classes, Symphony, Talent Show, etc.

7. Newspaper, Yearbook, Annual - Sponsoring, Supervising, and Chaperoning.

-Over-

8. Award Nights, Contests, May Day, Science Fair, Social Science Projects, Spelling Bee, TV Quiz, etc.

9. Baccalaureate, Class Night, Commencement, Ring Committee.

10. FUND RAISING ACTIVITIES:

   Candy, Car Washing, Doughnuts, Fun Night, Father-Son Ball Games, Plays, Popcorn, Paper Drives, Ribbon Sales, Sock Hops, Ticket Sales, etc.

11. SPECIAL CLASSES AND TUTORING:

   Art, For Absentees, For Accelerated, Ceramics, Crafts, Math, Music, Reading, For Under-achievers.

12. JANITORIAL SERVICES:

   Cleaning Blackboards, Dusting Tables and Counter Tops.

13. LIBRARY:

   Clerical Work - Preparation and distribution of library books.

   (* Unless teaching under the Smith-Hughes Act.)

   Your school may have activities similar to some of the above which should be included in this list. However, it should be remembered these activities are considered Extra-Curricular, Non-Compensated IF DONE BEFORE OR AFTER THE REGULARLY CONTRACTED SCHOOL DAY. The SCHOOL DAY is 15 MINUTES BEFORE THE OPENING OF SCHOOL AND 15 MINUTES AFTER DISMISSAL OF SCHOOL.

   > BUS DUTY AND SAFETY PATROL DUTY - You will note that these non-compensated activities are not included. The League recommends that teachers continue these activities, under protest only, because of the safety of children. These activities are items on which the League will make recommendations to the Administration soon.

   PLEASE KEEP THIS LIST FOR FUTURE REFERENCE

APPENDIX E

JOSEPHINE GOSS, ET AL.,   )
)
                    Plaintiffs   )
)
v.   )   No. 3984
)
THE BOARD OF EDUCATION OF THE CITY   )
OF KNOXVILLE, TENNESSEE, ET AL.,   )
)
                    DEFENDANTS   )

AMENDMENT TO PLAN OF DESEGREGATION OF THE BOARD OF EDUCATION
OF KNOXVILLE, TENNESSEE ADOPTED AUGUST, 1971

The plan of desegregation of the City of Knoxville, Tennessee is amended in the following respects.

   1.   The administration shall prepare and maintain a Pupil Locator Map. The first report should be available by October 1, 1971.

   2.   The Administration shall establish insofar as Administratively sound, school faculties and supporting personnel in each school with a ratio of Negroes to Whites as the school system as a whole. School personnel shall be assigned so that the racial composition of the staff shall in no way indicate that the school is intended for black or for white students.

   3.   The transfer criteria for transfer from an assigned school attendance zone to another school attendance zone within the school system shall be amended to read as follows:

        A.   Such transfers will be granted only for the following reasons:

             1.   Vocational education courses, Special Education program assignments, and/or preschool programs operated by the Board of Education.

             2.   Majority to minority race transfer.

        B.   Such transfers are effective for one school year and must be renewed annually. Transfers granted for vocational reasons will be honored only as long as the pupil pursues the stated vocational program.

165

C.   Such transfers will not be terminated for reasons of discipline.

4.   The following adjustments will be made in attendance zone lines as shown by the attached exhibit.

A.   Lonsdale and Sam E. Hill school attendance zones will be combined and the two school buildings paired. One building will provide an educational program for grades 1 - 3 and the other for grades 4 - 6.

B.   Close Cansler School as a regular day school dividing the students now attending Cansler with Beaumont and West View. The SMR Program at Beaumont will be transferred to Cansler.

C.   Close Moses Elementary School by moving the pre-school program to Cansler and the regular day students to Maynard. This would allow for an expansion of the Van Gilder Special Vocational Program.

D.   Elementary zones in East Knoxville involving Green, Eastport, Robert Huff and the new Sara Moore Green School remain the same until the new school is occupied in August, 1972 at which time the zone lines are as shown on the exhibit.

E.   Organize Beardsley Junior High School into a 7 - 8 school drawing students from the combined Rule-Beardsley attendance zones. Designate Rule as a 9 - 12 high school drawing students from the same area.

F.   Adjust the attendance zone lines between Holston and Austin-East High Schools as shown on exhibit.

G.   Pair the vocational programs of Austin-East and Fulton High Schools and extend transportation now available.

5. Majority to minority transfers are encouraged and within budget limitations the Board will consider transportation of students seeking such transfers.

6. A Biracial Committee shall be appointed to advise the Board of Education on current and future desegregation efforts. Members of the committee have been designated and the committee has been in many sessions exploring the school racial problems of Knoxville.

7. In the election of cheerleaders a student from a minority race of at least 5% or 50 students within a school may serve as a cheerleader if they receive the highest number of votes for a minority student regardless of the total votes cast in the election.

CERTIFICATE OF SERVICE

The undersigned hereby certifies that on the 1st day of September, 1971, this amendment was served upon the attorneys for each party affected thereby by mailing it to said attorneys at their last known address.

```
                                    Sam F. Fowler, Jr.
                                    Attorney for Defendants
```

SFFjr/mas

EXHIBIT TO AMENDMENT TO PLAN OF DESEGREGATION
OF THE BOARD OF EDUCATION OF KNOXVILLE,
TENNESSEE, ADOPTED AUGUST, 1971

Elementary Schools

1. It is recommended that Sam E. Hill and Lonsdale be paired. Place grades 1-3 in Sam E. Hill and grades 4-6 in Lonsdale. It is also recommended that the present zoning boundary along Vermont Avenue be enforced to require those students appropriately designated to attend the paired Sam E. Hill and Lonsdale complex.

2. It is recommended that Cansler Elementary School be closed. On eliminating Cansler, the West View zone should incorporate that portion of the Cansler zone from the corner of Western Avenue and Westview perpendicularly south to University (Myers, Century, Orange, Westview, Ambrister, Clinbrook, and Norman). The Beaumont zone should include the remainder of the Cansler zone.

   Approximately 100 students from Cansler will attend West View; the other 160 will be enrolled in Beaumont. As Beaumont is predominately white (857 White, 93 Black) and West View totally white, this tentative possibility--

regardless of the dimensions of the black-white
distribution---would not diametrically affect either
school.

3. It is recommended that Moses Elementary School--
1970-71 enrollment 169 White, 30 Black---be closed.
Students in the Moses zone residing south of the
I-40 Expressway (admittedly few) should attend Ft.
Sanders Elementary, students currently enrolled in
the Moses zone living north of the I-40 Expressway
should enroll in Maynard. Ft. Sanders and Maynard
are both theoretically amenable to increased student
numbers (approximately 150 and 100, respectively).

4. It is recommended that the Beaumont zone be extended
to include Exeter Street through Hooker Street,
requiring a high concentration of Black students now
enrolled in Maynard to enter Beaumont. With Maynard
receiving largely white students from Moses and losing
largely black students to Beaumont, the exaggerated
racial inequity should be reduced.

5. It is recommended that Robert Huff School be closed
when the proposed new elementary school opens as
scheduled in the fall of 1972. The present Green
zone, incorporating the defunct Mountain View zone,
will remain intact; the Eastport zone should emcompass

-2-

the area from Ontario Street south to the original
southern boundary below Delrose Drive and hence
including a considerable segment of the old Robert
Huff district; and the northern boundary of the
"new school district" will extend east along Wilson
Avenue continuing south on Ault Street to the
intersection of Lilac Avenue and Dunlap Lane
(approximately), with the original eastern boundary
of the new xschool to replace Robert Huff remaining
as is.

Junior High Schools

1. Beardsley Junior High School -

    It is recommended that zoning lines be shifted so
this school will be available to more white students.
Grades 7 and 8 at Rule should be moved to Beardsley
Junior High School. This would leave Rule with grades
9, 10, 11, and 12. The suggested Beardsley Junior
High School zone line should be University Avenue on
the south. Northern boundary should be the old zone
line.

2. Tyson Junior High School -

    It is recommended that the present school zone
be moved north from York Avenue to University Avenue.
This will help achieve the desired ratio between
black and white students.

3. Vine Junior High School -

    It is recommended that students east of Broadway
in the McCallie Elementary School zone attend Vine
Junior High School. It is also recommended that students
in the present Robert Huff area west of the corner of
Fern Street and Skyline Drive south to Boyd Bridge and
Delrose Drive also attend Vine Junior High School.

-4-

4. Christenberry Junior High School -

    It is recommended that students west of Broadway
    in the McCallie Elementary School zone attend
    Christenberry Junior High School. The northern
    boundary of this zone should be moved north from the
    present location to Dutch Valley Drive.

5. Park Junior High School -

    Enforcement of attendance utilizing present zone
    lines is recommended and would be a partial solution
    toward the desired ratio between black and white students.
    It is recommended that students east of Broadway in the
    Brownlow elementary area attend Park Junior High School.
    It is also recommended that students west of Fern
    Street extended north to the intersection of northeast
    boundary of zone lines in the Austin-East High School
    and south to the intersection of Fern Street and Skyline
    Drive also attend Park Junior High School.

6. Chilhowee School -

    It is recommended that students east of Fern
    Street, extended North and South attend Chilhowee School
    in grades 7 and 8 and Holston High School for grade 9.

-5-

High Schools

Of all the high schools only one, namely Austin-East High, reflects an undesirable integration balance of black and white students. It is, however, true; three junior high schools, situated within two high school zones, show a racial imbalance in their enrollment. These are Beardsley Jr., Park Jr., and Vine Jr. For that reason these junior high schools must also be considered when rezoning or pairing to bring about racial balance in the affected high schools.

For this reason two high school zones are considered as critical, namely Rule and Austin-East. The following are recommended:

I. Racial balance in the Rule zone

A consideration of the Rule zone includes focus on the Rule High School and the Beardsley Jr. High School where the present enrollments are:

Rule High: 996 White   304 Black
Beardsley Jr.:   81 White   339 Black

Keeping in mind the fact that a functional high school program requires a minimum of 900 students, we suggest the following:

A. Pairing Rule High and Beardsley Jr. High
    School as follows:

    1. Grades 7 and 8 at Beardsley Jr. High
        School.

    2. Grades 9, 10, 11, and 12 at Rule
        High School.

    It is anticipated that this will increase the
number of white students at Beardsley.

B. Adding to the Rule zone students from the Central
    High School area while also transferring the
    southern section of the Rule zone to the zone for
    the West High School and Tyson Jr. High Schools.

    It is anticipated that this will have the affect
· of increasing the white student population and decreasing
the black student population while, at the same time,
resulting in an overall increased student population for
the Rule zone. The proposed new southern boundary for
the Rule zone will be University Avenue running west
from I-75 to where it intersects the present eastern
zone for Rule.

II. The Austin-East and Fulton zones

     At present the Austin-East High School enrollment
figures are 782 black, 3 white. Keeping in mind that
· Austin-East offers vocational training and that a

-7-

functional high school program requires at least 900
students. The following recommendations are made:

A. Fulton and Austin-East be paired for vocational
    training purposes.

B. The area be rezoned to (1) increase the white
    student population, (2) decrease the black
    student population, and (3) increase the overall
    student population.

    It is suggested that the zone boundaries be as
follows:

A. Western--the existing boundary

B. Southern--the existing boundary eastward and
    continuing on the southern Holston boundary to
    the point just south of where Delrose Drive
    intersects with Boyd Bridge Drive.

C. Eastern boundary--a line extending northward
    from the corner of Magnolia Avenue and Fern
    Street to the point of intersection of the three
    present zone lines of Fulton/Austin-East, Fulton/
    Holston, and Holston/Austin-East.

D. A line extending southward along Fern Street from
    the corner until it meets the southern Holston
    zone line at the point where Delrose Drive and
    Boyd Bridge Drive meet.

E. Northern Boundary--the existing boundary.

Furthermore, inasmuch as a section from the Fulton
zone is removed to Austin-East and a large new township
is proposed north of the present northern boundary for
Fulton, it is recommended that the Fulton area be rezoned.
The northern boundary of this zone should be moved north
of the present location so that Dutch Valley Drive becomes
the northern boundary running from I-75 to the point where
the present Fulton/Central, Fulton/Holston, and Central
boundaries intersect.

-9-

APPENDIX F

MEMBERS OF THE KNOXVILLE BOARD OF EDUCATION WHO SERVED DURING THE YEARS OF DESEGREGATION LITIGATION, 1954–1974

	YEARS SERVED
Victor E. Arning Jr.	1964–1968
Kenneth Bailes	1970–1986
Earl G. Bond	1974–1978
H. L. Bradley	1952–1956
Charles R. Burchett	1968–1975
Dr. John H. Burkhart	1958–1962
W. Hoyle Campbell	1942–1958
J. W. Carty	1970–1984
Marion (Mrs. Robert S.) Chapman	1962–1966
D. A. Cooper	1954–1958
Jack L. Cooper	1972–1974
Lynn W. Craig	1966–1970
W. M. Davis	1972–1974
Bayard C. Erskine	1970–1974
Wallace Frazier	1948–1956
Sarah Moore Greene	1970–1986
Lewis S. Howard	1968–1972
John S. Humphreys	1966–1978
Andrew Johnson	1954–1958
Mary Ellen (Mrs. Gilmer) Keith	1958–1962
Roy E. Linville	1960–1964
Dr. Charles Moffett	1958–1962
Dr. Bergein F. Overholt	1972–1978
Robert B. Ray	1956–1964
Alex A. Shafer	1962–1966
W. Howard Temple	1964–1976
Julia M. Tucker	1974–1982
E. C. Woods	1956–1960
Luther Woods	1970–1971

NOTES

CHAPTER 1

1. Tennessee Advisory Committee to the United States Commission on Civil Rights Report, *School Desegregation in Tennessee: 12 Districts Released from Desegregation Orders, 17 Under Court Jurisdiction*, April 2008, p. 1.

2. Ibid.

3. Ibid., p. 2.

4. Knoxville Board of Education minutes, July 12, 1954.

5. *Knoxville News-Sentinel*, July 10, 1954.

6. Defendants-Appellees' brief, No. 14,425, in the United States Court of Appeals for the Sixth District.

7. Board minutes, August 17, 1955. Knox County Archives.

8. Tennessee Advisory Committee to United States Commission on Civil Rights Report, April 2008, p. 10.

9. Defendants-Appellees' brief, No.14,425, p. 4.

10. Personal files, Fred Bedelle.

11. Memorandum opinion, August 19, 1960, p. 2.

12. *Knoxville Journal*, May 15, 1956.

13. *Dianne Ward et al. v. The Board of Education of the City of Knoxville, Tennessee, et al.* petition, January 7, 1957, p. 5.

14. Ibid., p.8.

15. *Knoxville Journal*, January 13, 1957.

16. *Knoxville News-Sentinel*, January 14, 1957.

17. Ibid., February 27, 1957.

18. Board minutes, January 9, 1957.

19. Ibid., January 18, 1957.

20. Answer filed by Frank Fowler to *Ward* complaint, June 28, 1957.

21. Ibid.

22. Ibid.

23. Interview with Theotis Robinson Jr.

24. Interview with Raleigh Wynn.

25. Interview with Ruth Benn.

26. Court docket, National Archives.

27. Board minutes, January 1, 1959.

28. Personal files, Frank Fowler.

29. Court docket, National Archives.

CHAPTER 2

1. *Knoxville News-Sentinel*, January 3, 1960.

2. *Knoxville Journal*, January 27, 1960.

3. *Knoxville News-Sentinel*, January 27, 1960.

4. Ibid., February 8, 1960.

5. Ibid.

6. *Knoxville Journal*, March 20, 1960.

7. Ibid.

8. Ibid.

9. Ibid.

10. *Knoxville News-Sentinel*, March 31, 1960.

11. Ibid.

12. Board minutes, March 30, 1960.

13. Ibid., April 4, 1960.

14. Ibid.

15. *Knoxville Journal*, April 5, 1960.

16. *Knoxville News-Sentinel*, April 5, 1960.

17. Ibid., April 18, 1960.

18. Ibid.

19. *Josephine Goss et al. v. The Board of Education of the City of Knoxville, Tennessee, et al.,* 340 F. Supp 711 (1972).

20. *Knoxville News-Sentinel*, April 5, 1960.

21. Memorandum opinion of Judge Taylor, Civil Order Book 19, p. 339.

22. 279 F. Supp. 903.

23. Plaintiffs' Specifications of Objections, April 10, 1961.

24. Defendants' response to objections, June 14, 1961.

25. *Knoxville News-Sentinel*, June 6, 1961.

26. Ibid.

27. Ibid., June 12, 1961.

28. Ibid., July 20, 1961.

29. Opinion rendered from the bench, June 19, 1961.

30. Ibid.

31. Ibid.

32. Ibid.

33. Court docket, National Archives.

CHAPTER 3

1. Personal files, Frank Fowler.

2. Court of Appeals decision, Nashville, TN, April, 4, 1962.

3. Memo from clerk, Carl W. Reuss, April 18, 1962.

4. Personal files, Frank Fowler.

5. Ibid.

6. Ibid.

7. Court docket, National Archives.

8. Personal files, Frank Fowler.

9. Plan submitted to court. (See appendix B.)

10. Court docket, National Archives.

11. Plaintiffs' Specifications of Objections, September 19, 1962.

12. Reply of defendant to Specifications of Objections to amended plan, October 16, 1962.

13. Board minutes, December 10, 1962.

14. *Knoxville News-Sentinel*, October 11, 1962.

15. Letter from Frank Fowler to Thomas Johnston, November 1, 1962. Personal files, Frank Fowler.

16. Board minutes, March 11, 1963.

17. Ibid.

18. Plaintiffs' Specifications of Objections, March 28, 1963.

19. *Knoxville News-Sentinel*, March 21, 1963.

20. Ibid.

21. 270 F. Supp. 1967.

22. Court docket, National Archives.

23. Civil Order Book 24, p. 67.

24. Personal files, Frank Fowler.

25. Board minutes, May 13, 1963.

26. *Knoxville News-Sentinel*, September 2, 1962.

27. Ibid., September 4, 1962.

28. National Archives, Order Book 28, p. 184.

29. Board minutes, May 15, 1964,
30. *Knoxville News-Sentinel*, May 12, 1964.
31. *Knoxville Journal*, May 12, 1964.
32. *Josephine Goss v. Knoxville Board of Education*, National Archives, June 11, 1964.
33. Ibid., October 29,1964.
34. National Commission of Professional Rights and Responsibilities of the National Education Association of the United States, *Knoxville, Tennessee: When a City Government Fails to Give Full Support to its Schools*, March 1977.
35. 270 F. Supp. 903,918.

CHAPTER 4

1. Personal files, Frank Fowler.
2. Motion for Pre-trial Conference, January 21, 1965, National Archives.
3. Personal files, Frank Fowler.
4. Ibid.
5. Agreed Order, February 12, 1965.
6. Board minutes, February 8, 1965.
7. Specifications of Objections, National Archives.
8. *Knoxville News-Sentinel*, April 30, 1965.
9. *Knoxville Journal*, May 4, 1965.
10. Further Specifications of Objections filed June 18, 1965, National Archives.
11. *Knoxville Journal*, July 29, 1965.
12. Ibid.
13. Ibid.
14. Agreed Order, July 28, 1965
15. *Knoxville News-Sentinel*, July 29, 1965.
16. Civil Order Book 33, p.192, National Archives.
17. *Knoxville Journal*, July 31, 1965.
18. *Knoxville News-Sentinel*, July 31, 1965.

19. Board of education plan submitted August 6, 1965.
20. *Knoxville News-Sentinel*, August 12, 1965.
21. Ibid., August 18, 1965.
22. Ibid.
23. Board minutes, August 23, 1965.
24. Personal files, Frank Fowler.
25. Ibid.
26. Ibid.
27. Personal files, Fred Bedelle.
28. *Knoxville News-Sentinel*, December 6, 1966.
29. Pre-trial Order, March 10, 1967.
30. Memorandum Opinion, June 7, 1967.
31. Board minutes, February 12, 1968.
32. Ibid., April 15, 1968.

CHAPTER 5

1. Personal files, Sam Fowler.
2. Carl Cowan files, Knox County Archives.
3. *Knoxville News-Sentinel*, December 7, 1969.
4. Ibid.
5. Plaintiff's Motion to Dismiss, February 17, 1970.
6. Personal files, Sam Fowler.
7. Personal files, Fred Bedelle.
8. Ibid.
9. Personal files, Sam Fowler.
10. *Knoxville Journal*, March 10, 1970.
11. Ibid.
12. Judge Taylor's order, March 16, 1970.
13. *Knoxville News-Sentinel*, April 6, 1970.
14. Personal files, Sam Fowler.
15. Motion to Amend, April 13, 1970. National Archives.
16. Personal files, Sam Fowler.

17. National Archives, objection to Motion for Production of Documents, May 4, 1970.

18. Personal files, Sam Fowler.

19. Ibid.

20. Ibid.

21. *Goss* court docket, July 22, 1970. Order Book 53, p. 174, National Archives.

22. Bernstein, Brittany, "All Deliberate Delay: Desegregating the Public Schools of Orange County Schools." *University of Central Florida Undergraduate Research Journal*, 2005.

23. *Knoxville Journal*, August 11, 1970.

24. *Knoxville News-Sentinel*, August 25, 1970.

25. Ibid., August 30, 1970.

26. Ibid., August 31, 1970.

27. Board minutes, June 14, 1971.

28. *Bradley v. School District of City of Richmond, Virginia, 325 F.Supp., 828, April 5, 1971.*

29. Board minutes, July 12, 1971.

30. United States Court of Appeals, 444 F.2d 632.

31. The pupil locator map was prepared on the kitchen floor at the home of the assistant superintendent, Dr. Fred Bedelle Jr., with the aide of his family. Of all the records produced for this court case, this map could not be located.

32. Court docket, July 1, 1971.

33. Ibid., July 6, 1971.

34. Ibid., July 9, 1971.

35. *Knoxville News-Sentinel*, August 5, 1971.

36. Ibid., August 10, 1971.

37. Board Minutes, August 23, 1971.

38. Ibid., August 16, 1971.

39. *Knoxville Journal*, August 26, 1971.

40. Personal files, Sam Fowler.

41. *Knoxville News-Sentinel*, August 16, 1971.

42. Ibid.

43. Ibid.

44. Ibid. August 18, 1971.

45. Ibid. August 19, 1971.

46. Ibid. August 24, 1971.

47. *Knoxville Journal*, August 19, 1971.

48. *Knoxville News-Sentinel*, August 24, 1971.

CHAPTER 6

1. National Archives, Civil Action 3984, January 20, 1972.

2. Personal files, Sam Fowler.

3. *Knoxville News-Sentinel*, January 31, 1972.

4. Ibid., February 2, 1972.

5. Ibid.

6. Ibid.

7. Transcript of hearing, February 1–3, 1972.

8. *Knoxville News-Sentinel*, February 1, 1972.

9. Ibid., February 2, 1972.

10. Personal files, Sam Fowler.

11. Ibid.

12. *Knoxville Journal*, March 10, 1972.

13. Opinion of US Court of Appeals, August 16, 1973.

14. Brake, Patricia, *Justice in the Valley*, (Hillsboro Press: Franklin, TN, 1998), 125.

15. *Goss*, 186 F.Supp. 559 (D.C. Tenn. 1960), p. 11.

INDEX

Bold page numbers indicate that the entry is found in a caption.

ABOUT THE AUTHOR

F red Bedelle Jr. received his EdD from the University of Tennessee and worked for over fifty years in education. He served twenty-eight years in various administrative positions in the public schools of Knoxville and Knox County, Tennessee. His last position in public education was as the superintendent of the Knoxville City Schools.

As the director of research and development in the mid-1960s, Dr. Bedelle was assigned the task of representing the Knoxville Board of Education at court hearings and explaining federal compliance issues and the court's school desegregation orders to the board with regard to the case of *Josephine Goss, et al. v. The Board of Education of the City of Knoxville, Tennessee.*

For the next twenty-three years after leaving his position as super intendent, Dr. Bedelle worked as a graduate faculty member and, eventually, dean of the Carter and Moyers School of Education at Lincoln Memorial University in Harrogate, Tennessee. He retired in April 2010, and was awarded the status of dean emeritus.

Dr. Bedelle and his wife, Norma, are now enjoying retirement in Knoxville, Tennessee.